Prayer and Our Bodies

Prayer
and
Our
Bodies

Flora Slosson Wuellner

THE UPPER ROOM
Nashville, Tennessee

Prayer and Our Bodies

Copyright © 1987 Flora Slosson Wuellner. All rights reserved.

No part of this book may be reproduced in any manner whatsoever without written permission of the publisher except in brief quotations embodied in critical articles or reviews. For information, address The Upper Room, 1908 Grand Avenue, P.O. Box 189, Nashville, Tennessee 37202.

The poem by Madeleine L'Engle is copyright © 1957, 1985 by Madeleine L'Engle. From A WINTER'S LOVE.

We gratefully acknowledge Bear & Company for permission to quote from the following books:
MEDITATIONS WITH JULIAN OF NORWICH, copyright © 1983 by Bear & Company, Inc.;
MEDITATIONS WITH HILDEGARD OF BINGEN, copyright © 1983 by Bear & Company, Inc.; and
MEDITATIONS WITH MECHTILD OF MAGDEBURG, copyright © 1982 by Bear & Company, Inc.

Scripture quotations not otherwise identified are from the Revised Standard Version of the Bible, copyrighted 1946, 1952, and © 1971 by the Division of Christian Education, National Council of Churches of Christ in the United States of America, and are used by permission.

Scripture quotations designated NEB are from *The New English Bible,* © The Delegates of the Oxford University Press 1961 and 1970, and are used by permission.

Scripture paraphrases identified as such are taken from *The Living Bible* (Wheaton, Illinois: Tyndale House Publishers, 1971) and are used by permission.

Book Design: Steve Laughbaum

First Printing: November 1987 (10)
Second Printing: November 1989 (3)
Third Printing: April 1990 (7)

Library of Congress Catalog Card Number: 87-050705
ISBN: 0-8358-0568-9

Printed in the United States of America

*Dedicated to my students at Pacific School of Religion
and the Graduate Theological Union,
from whom I have learned so much.*

Contents

Introduction

To write a book on the relationship of prayer to our bodies is a risky and presumptuous task. Such a book can easily become complacent and simplistic in describing our encounter with the mystery of our bodily selves. Even with all good intentions, extra burdens of guilt and expectation are all too easily laid on those already burdened with disease and bodily impairment.

There are no easy, glib rules and answers. Our understanding and awareness of our bodily selves unfold slowly as we grow, learn, and mature within God's embrace. As Christians we are taught that God has created our bodies and honors them. As Christians we try to abide in Jesus Christ, whose passion for healing and wholeness was a major part of his ministry. But still there is much mystery, much that is bewildering and unknown about our bodily selves, many answers that we simply do not yet have.

Can this perhaps be because God wishes not so much to *give* us answers as to have us *grow* into answers? When answers are given us before we are ready, they do not answer. This may be especially true of the mysterious interweaving between what we call our spirits and what we call our bodies. When the body is mentioned in the New Testament, it is often referred to by the Greek word *soma*, which usually implies the *whole* human self: body, emotion, intelligence, will. It is impossible to write a book on the body from the Christian standpoint and not include the emotions, the personality, the spirit, just as it is impossible to write a book on our emotions or our spirituality and not include the body. Because our faith is rooted in the incarnation of Jesus, any form of spirituality we claim must also be *incarnational*, which by definition includes the wholeness of the person. This will profoundly influence our relationship to our communities and our world.

This is not a book primarily about spiritual healing, though the suggested attitudes, responses, and prayers for and with the body may well result in healing. And certainly this is not a book in which rules are prescribed for physical habits, diet, weight control, exercise, sexual behavior, or community or ecological involvement! I believe strongly that as we grow into a new, transforming relationship with our bodily selves, we will begin spontaneously and naturally to make informed decisions about our habits, lifestyles, and relationships.

This book is also not meant to replace any needed medical or psychological treatment and therapy. Rather, it is meant to be read and used as an enriching accompaniment to any necessary medical therapy. The book does not presume to replace the nurture, healing, and guidance that can be found in a church family, the body of Christ on earth, through which our *soma*, our whole physical, emotional, relational selves, are encountered, embraced, and empowered.

Rather, the purpose of this book is to explore and suggest ways by which we can experience a healed enrichment and wholeness as children of God through a transformed relationship with our bodily selves. Such transformation is not limited to our personal selves, but might also include a new understanding of the bodies of our communities and the body of our earth and of our relationship with them.

This book can be used by individuals and by groups. The suggested meditations can be experienced alone or in group context, although I urge any group to respect the privacy, reticences, and timing of its individual members. Some readers might prefer to read the book all the way through first and then to return to sections that seem especially relevant and helpful. Others may wish to move slowly through all the chapters, experiencing them and experimenting over a longer period of time. Some readers may wish to tape or record the suggested meditations in this book so that they may play them through, stopping at any point to focus and center on the experience. In order that these meditations may be a wholistic, creative experience, whether as a leader or participant, alone or in a group, the reader is urged to read the suggested guidelines in Appendices 1 and 2.

Any book, no matter how helpful, is only the witness of the author's personal belief and experience. Suggestions are given, alternatives offered, and experiences shared. The only thing that matters is what you, the reader, begin to hear, experience, discover about yourself as you, along with your body, grow ever more deeply in the love of God. The paraphrase of Ephesians 3:17-19 in *The Living Bible* expresses with power the longing and the promise.

May your roots go down deep into the soil of God's marvelous love; and may you be able to feel and understand, as all God's children should, how long, how wide, how deep, and how high his love really is; and to experience this love for yourselves, though it is so great that you will never see the end of it or fully know or understand it. And so at last you will be filled with God himself.

· 1 ·

Who Are Our Bodies?

"Let me tell you the very first dream I can remember," said my friend. We were sitting together in my study, which doubles as my counseling room. My friend, a gentle middle-aged woman, occasionally came to me for counseling.

"I must have been about four years old, maybe younger. But I remember it clearly. I was riding a tricycle along the sidewalk of a residential area, riding very slowly. I knew that I would soon come to a house that I was supposed to enter. When I approached the house, it looked like it was looming over me, though it wasn't actually all that big. It had a curving sidewalk and a nice little garden. It looked neat and well built. There was nothing wrong with it, but I was frightened anyway. I came closer and closer and then stopped and looked at it for a long time. Nothing happened. Suddenly I turned my tricycle around and peddled away as fast as I could. I felt a desperate need to *escape* from that house."

She hesitated, smiling a little. "I've heard that a child's first dreams or first memories are usually connected with the way she feels about her body. Around that age, children begin to be aware of their bodies objectively. I wonder if that first dream means that I was afraid of my body . . . in some way."

We sat in silence thinking this over. I remembered lying in my crib, playing with my fingers, occasionally trying to take them off. I also remembered a few years later when I went through an anxious, mercifully short phase when I would wake at night to be sure my heart was still beating and my breath was still breathing.

"I really felt responsible and alarmed about that," I shared with my friend.

"How did we get on this subject, anyway?" she asked, perplexed. "We had been talking about spiritual problems. Why are we suddenly talking about our bodies?"

A short silence, and then suddenly she said, "This *is* a spiritual matter. I think the way we feel about our bodies *is* somehow connected with our spirituality. I'm wondering if there's something about the mixed-up way I feel about my body that's important for me to understand . . . something God wants me to think about."

This conversation was a curious coincidence for me. For the last few months, a challenge had been coming to me from many different directions.

"When are you going to start teaching about our spiritual relationship to the *body*?" some of my students began to ask restlessly. "Sometimes you talk as if we were a lot of disembodied personalities sitting, no, floating around!"

"Sometimes your guided meditations make me feel light-headed. I don't feel *grounded*," a retreat member complained.

Books on the power and mystery of the body somehow kept coming my way. I found I was instinctively doing a lot of reading and thinking in this area. New images and symbols began to surface in my dreams and meditations.

This was puzzling. Certainly I had never meant to

14

exclude the body from my teaching on our spiritual encounters with emotional wounds and memories. During retreats, I always had a few kind words to say about the body, and had developed some guided prayers and meditations for physical relaxation. But, it was true. The body was always an afterthought, a sideline.

"All right, then, what *is my body*?" I began to ask in my prayers. An answer of sure and gentle strength seemed to rise from a deep place, not in words, but in strong, guided thought: "You are asking the wrong question."

I thought this over. The discomfort seemed to focus on that word *what*. *But what is wrong with that?* I thought defensively. *Aren't I a soul, a spirit, a personality who owns a body and controls (or tries to) the complex machinery of the physical self?* Was this the wrong interpretation? Was I trying to manipulate my body and therefore depersonalizing it?

"All right, then," I responded, "Then *who* is my body?" Again I sensed a gentle, and now amused, response into my conscious thoughts: "Why don't you ask your body that question?"

I have long believed that one way by which we can discern true guidance from God is by the combination of surprise and naturalness we feel. Indeed, I was surprised now. I had lived with my body for over half a century, and never once had I thought to speak to it directly, much less to listen for its answer! And yet, how strangely right and natural it seemed.

"Is this really a part of prayer?" I asked cautiously. "Am I wandering off into distractions?"

"Dear one," the tender response rose within me (did I *really* sense laughter?), "there *are* no distractions in prayer. Everything that rises in your heart when you speak to me is there for a good reason. Speak to your body now, in my presence, and ask directly who it is."

I focused on my bodily self, sitting so quietly in the chair: "Who are you?"

Responses rose so swiftly and urgently into my conscious mind that I was almost overwhelmed. They came like answers that had been pent up for years.

"I am your friend and closest partner. Sometimes I am your mother and father. Sometimes I am your child. Always I am your lover and spouse.

"I am the truth-teller. I witness to you your unknown self.

"I am the faithful messenger and recorder of your memories, your powers, your hurts, your needs, your limits.

"I am the stored wisdom and hurts of the ages and generations before you.

"I am a gift-giver. Through me, you live and move in God's creation. Through me, you have your vital link with the rejoicing, groaning, travailing universe.

"I am your partner in stress and pain. I carry much of your suffering, so your spirit does not need to carry it all alone.

"I am the frontier you have barely explored and the eager companion who speaks to you every moment.

"I am the manifestation of the miracle which is you. I am the ground of your deep powers.

"I am the microcosm of the community that surrounds you. I am the microcosm of the universe in which you live.

"I am the visible means by which you relate and unite with others.

"I am one of the major ways by which God abides with you, speaks to you, touches you, unites with you.

Who are you, body? (handwritten margin note)

"Far from separating you from your spiritual life, I open it to you.

"You can pray with me, for me, through me. I can pray also, in my way, when you cannot.

"I am always in embrace with you, though sometimes you ignore me or even hate and try to harm me.

"I will never leave you. I will be with you after death as your risen companion of clearer light and swifter energy in a different form. Only my outer appearance dies.

"Together, in passionate unity, we will become the fully alive human being."

I sat almost stunned at the door that suddenly had opened before me. Never, until now, had I thought of my body as a companion to be loved and heard, nurturingly, passionately, discerningly. I realized I could never go back again. No longer could my body be to me a prison of my spirit, a beast of burden to be driven, a machine to be manipulated, an opponent to be feared and resisted, a force to be subdued, a slave for my habits, or an instrument to be possessed. God was revealing to me the hidden but deeply responsive companion of my life's spiritual journey; the one whom many years ago I had wedded "for better, for worse, for richer, for poorer, in sickness and in health, as long as we both shall live."

A whole new and exciting spiritual adventure was opening before me. Where would it lead, now that I began at last to recognize and love my dear companion, the body? What new ways of praying would I discover? What new ways of living and relating? Along with the swift answers had come even more mysteries and perplexing questions. But isn't that what growing in love is all about?

Prayer and Our Bodies

Meditative Reading

The Word became flesh and dwelt among us, full of grace and truth.

—John 1:14

The creation itself will be set free from its bondage to decay and obtain the glorious liberty of the children of God.

—Romans 8:21

Excerpts of three meditations from Julian of Norwich of the fourteenth century:

As the body is clothed in cloth
and the muscles in the skin
and the bones in the muscles
and the heart in the chest,

so are we, body and soul,
clothed in the Goodness of God
and enclosed.

God is the means
whereby our Substance
and our Sensuality
are kept together
so as to never be apart.

Because of the beautiful oneing
that was made by God
between the body and the soul

it must be
that we will be restored
from double death.[1]

• 2 •

Reconciling and Celebrating with Our Bodies

We pray constantly for peace in our homes, our communities, and our world. Why are we so often at war with our bodies?

"I hate my body!" I recently heard a friend say. "It's no better than secondhand goods. I'd like to trade it in for a new model!"

I recently read an informal survey reporting almost 80 percent of women dislike their bodies or at least many parts of their bodies. How often do we look in the mirror and think: *I wish I had a different face, I wish my eyes were a different color, I hate the shape of my legs,* or, *I'm too big . . . I'm too thin . . . too fat . . . too short?*

Some of us jog or exercise to the point of punishment. Some of us take diet pills or go on crash diets to "get rid of that ugly fat." We blame our stomachs for our eating problems, and we blame our sexual systems for our sexual behavior. When our bodies get ill or tired, we blame them for letting us down. When they are well, we take them for granted.

Many of us carry around unhealed inner hurts about our bodily, and therefore our emotional, selves. Perhaps our families and school friends teased or rejected us because we were hyperactive, slow in sports, clumsy

19

with our hands, too tall, too short, too plump, or too skinny.

We spend a lifetime centered around the necessities of feeding, clothing, and sheltering our bodies, and we anxiously or impatiently take them to doctors when we are sick. But we almost never think about them in *depth* or listen thoughtfully to their signals of stress and distress.

Our western culture almost brainwashes us into helplessness, anger, anxiety at the great physical transitions of life: adolescence, middle life, menopause, aging, and death. At these times, for many of us, our bodies are at best puzzling, scary machines out of control or at worst malevolent, treacherous enemies.

What have our bodies done to us that we ignore, dislike, and punish them so? Do we merely aim for self-improvement, better health, and beauty? If so, these qualities (as we know with our children and even our pets and plants) flourish best in an atmosphere of warm friendliness, encouragement, respect, communication, and sensitivity to ability and timing. It is far more likely that much unhealed anger, fear, and hurt underlies our dislike and suspicion of our bodily selves. For many of us, our bodies are the victims of our loneliness, anxiety, and our need to control our environment.

Is this not the same underlying fear and hurt that exists among our families, communities, and warring nations? Is it possible that God is able to begin the reconciling, transforming work here in our own bodily selves?

There are many hopeful and joyful signs that the reconciling work has begun. There are new, more wholistic ways of eating and drinking; there are new, helpful ways of taking charge of our bodies in illness and medical treatment; alternatives are now offered for childbirth, the middle years, and the challenges of aging. But these changes are still very much on the frontiers of our thinking and living. They have not yet taken deep root in our culture.

This is not only a cultural concern, but a spiritual concern. The way we relate to our bodily selves profoundly influences the way we relate to God, to one another, to prayer, to all of life.

Unfortunately, there is still a widespread mindset in many churches and Christian communities that our bodies are *hindrances* to our spiritual lives. It is still too often implied, if not actually taught, that the body is, by its very nature, lower, inferior, separating us from God. Some of our most loved hymns reinforce this concept, such as the beautiful hymn by Whittier, "Dear Lord and Father of Mankind," in which the last verse urges: "Let sense be dumb, let flesh retire." This seems to confirm the ancient heresy that the flesh is a prison in which the spirit is trapped and tempted. But this concept is not the incarnational, biblical witness.

A careful reading of Paul's epistles clears up many misunderstandings. For example, in his letter to the church in Galatia, in which he contrasts the works of the flesh and the works of the Spirit, we see that the problems he lists as belonging to the flesh include many things which are not especially related to the body at all: "idolatry, sorcery, enmity, strife, jealousy, anger, selfishness, party spirit, envy" (5:20-21). It is obvious that Paul means by flesh not the body itself, but the fragmented, sinful condition of the *whole* person who is not yet healed and transformed by Christ.

Paul's basic teaching about the body is clearly stated in his letter to the church in Corinth: "Do you not know that your bodies are members of Christ? . . . Do you not know that your body is a temple of the Holy Spirit

21

within you which you have from God? . . . Glorify God in your body" (1 Cor. 6:15, 19-20).

With equal power, he wrote to the church at Philippi: "It is my eager expectation and hope that I shall not be at all ashamed, but that with full courage . . . Christ will be honored in my body whether by life or by death" (1:20).

The witness of Jesus is stated simply and completely in John's Gospel: "Jesus answered them, 'Destroy this temple, and in three days I will raise it up.' . . . He spoke of the temple of his body" (2:19, 21).

Throughout the Bible, we see many perplexities of the body, many sufferings in the body, but *always* the triumphant affirmation that "God saw everything that [God] had made, and behold, it was very good" (Gen. 1:31).

If God created, loved, and honored our bodies and so blessed them by the incarnation, then our bodily selves were meant to be to us priceless, incomparable gifts.

This does not mean that we are to idolize our bodies or obey every physical impulse or abandon attempts to improve health and appearance. Nor does it mean that we may never have to compel or even sacrifice our bodies for love of others. Rather, it means that we are to be healed of our dislike for our bodies. We are to learn to listen to the signals of our bodies, honoring them as one of the main ways God speaks to us and by which we can learn much unencountered truth about ourselves and our communities.

Who is this "I" or "we" that listens to and dialogues with our bodies? Certainly it is not some "ghost in the machine" or some spiritual entity hovering above the ground. The "I" is our *conscious* self, the perceiver, the interpreter. It is not detached from the body or the deep self; it is like an island that is the only visible part of an underwater mountain range or a ray of light from a lighthouse that focuses on specific parts of the surrounding mystery of darkness.

When I speak of relationship with the body, I do not deny the oneness and unity of our whole selves, for that would be unwholistic fragmentation and compartmentalization. But a healing process can result from the focus on our various physical and emotional aspects as if they were beings in themselves. By thus visualizing and communicating in prayer with these "identities" of our bodies and feelings, we often experience deepening healing and unity. Fragmentation results when we are *out* of touch with our emotions and bodies. Through encountering these two aspects of ourselves with awareness and love, they become increasingly unified, vital parts of our whole selves. This relationship between our conscious selves and our bodily selves was meant to be exciting, enjoyable, trustful, alert, and nurturing, with each part sharing its own special gifts and powers.

The first step in this new marriage of our powers is often the healing and forgiveness for the wounds of contempt and compulsion. If for years we have disliked, ignored, or repudiated parts of our bodies, quite possibly the level of consciousness in every cell and organ has picked up these thoughts and feelings. We know that even very young children pick up our attitudes, and there is much evidence that this is also true of our pets and plants; so shouldn't this also be true of the living cells of our bodies? And what has this done to us over the years?

We should not pretend or try to force ourselves to love what we do not love. That can do even more harm. But we can face our true feelings and pray that the anxiety or anger that underlies the feelings may be healed. We can pray for awareness that our disliked bodily parts *are* part of us and have served us faithfully. We can stop blaming our bodies for our own decisions. For example, it is *I*, not my stomach, who decides what I will eat and drink. My stomach sends out signals of distress at my decision and is the victim, not the perpetrator. We can pray for awareness of the deep mystery of our bodily selves. It is helpful to think of our bodies as microcosms of our whole earth, even of our universe. I recently came across a glorious little poem by Madeleine L'Engle:

> I am fashioned as a galaxy,
> Not as a solid substance but a mesh
> Of atoms in their far complexity
> Forming the pattern of my bone and flesh.
>
> Small solar systems are my eyes.
> Muscle and sinew are composed of air.
> Like comets flashing through the evening skies
> My blood runs, ordered, arrogant, and fair.
>
> Ten lifetimes distant is the nearest star,
> And yet within my body, firm as wood,
> Proton and electron separate are.
> Bone is more fluid than my coursing blood.
> What plan had God, so strict and so empassioned
> When He an island universe my body fashioned?[2]

Such awareness of the awesome mystery of our bodily selves is one of the first ways to encounter the vaster mystery of God.

We can learn from a loving family or any other group bonded in tenderness how to respond to the signals of distress or hurt from our bodies. We all know how one crying, distressed child involves the whole family in

24

concern—in a healthy family. It is the same with our bodies: contempt of even one small part is deeply damaging to the whole. Celebration of even one small part is deeply healing to the whole. In his comparison of the human body to the human community, Paul writes:

> The body does not consist of one member but of many. . . . If all were a single organ, would the body be? . . . The eye cannot say to the hand, "I have no need of you." . . . On the contrary, the parts of the body which seem to be weaker are indispensable, and those parts of the body which we think less honorable we invest with the greater honor. . . . If one member suffers, all suffer together; if one member is honored, all rejoice together.
> —1 Corinthians 12:14, 19, 21-23, 26

How can we begin our own reconciliation with our bodies? Try a deliberate encounter with some bodily part you have ignored or disliked. Maybe you have always been somewhat ashamed of your hands, their size or shape. Look at your hands and inwardly speak to them, somewhat in this manner: "Dear friends, you have served me faithfully every day of my life. I do my work and I touch other people and the world around me through you. Forgive me that I've been ashamed of you. I'd like to learn to *rejoice* in you!"

If you have taken the service of your eyes for granted recently, try to take a moment occasionally to lean back, place your palms gently and warmly over your eyes, praise them for their service, and encourage them in their work.

If this inner communicating seems uncomfortable and embarrassing at first, it is enough just to glance at your hands in a friendly way and thank God for them or think of your eyes occasionally and praise God for the gift they are.

As you encounter the suggested meditations I give in this book, feel free to use, discard, or make substitutes for any symbolism, imagery, or procedure that does not feel right for you. The Bible is full of helpful symbols of the love of God. I use the symbol of light a great deal; but wind, water, mountains, green pastures, shepherd, mother, father, bridegroom, and many other symbols are equally biblical. Ask God to bring to your heart what is right for *you*. You will probably find that what is right changes in time. If you don't like visualizing, it is enough to ask, claim, and give thanks that God is close to you, loving and healing you. Whatever method you choose, remember that Christ is not running around doing our bidding. God's love and light forever embrace us whether we pray or not. But through prayer we are consenting, claiming, and *internalizing God's offered healing*, which then becomes empowered in our lives and bodies.

Suggested Meditation of Reconciliation with Your Body

Do you not know that your body is a temple of the Holy Spirit within you . . .? Glorify God in your body.
—1 Corinthians 6:19-20

In a comfortable, relaxed position, think of God's nearness and love around you, flowing through you like warm light, color, water, or wind; or think of God's love coming to you through Jesus or some person whom you love and trust. If inner visualization is not helpful to you, hold something in your hand that helps you relax and center; listen to music or birds singing; smell a flower or incense; or, best of all, call on the name of Jesus Christ, who is forever near you, longing to heal you.

Gently breathe, and pay attention to the breathing. Think of each breath as the breath of life from God. Sense the healing light flowing into your body with each breath.

Think of some part of your body that you have disliked or of which you have been ashamed. Picture that part being touched lovingly by Jesus Christ, or picture that bodily part being gently washed by the healing light.

Lay your own hands on that part of your body if you comfortably can. In your own words, thank it for being a faithful friend in spite of your dislike; or, just thank God for that bodily part and its service. Ask to be healed of your dislike.

Think of some part of your body that is under stress, uncomfortable, in pain, or undergoing some other problem. Touch it if you can, thank it both for undertaking healing tasks for your whole body and for helping carry the hurts and burdens of your spirit. Thank God for this bodily part, its hard work, and ask to be shown how to listen to its signals and how you can best help it in its work.

Now think of a part of your body which you have ignored and taken for granted. Touch it with your hands or with your thoughts; thank it; praise it for its faithfulness and its value to your whole body.

Think of one of your organic systems: respiratory, circulatory, digestive, reproductive, and so forth. Picture its general area of work in your body. Send it loving, encouraging thoughts, and picture God's living stream of light flowing through that system, renewing it. Give thanks for its faithful service.

Try to remember your very first memory of your body as a child. Was it a warm, friendly memory? If so, give thanks for that beginning. If it is a memory of shame, fear, pain, or discomfort, ask for the healing of that time. Let Jesus hold and comfort that small body which was yours.

Think of some moment in your life when someone else repudiated you or teased you because of the way your body looked or moved. See your bodily self as a child, teenager, or adult embraced, comforted, valued by God.

Face the bodily time of your life now. Thank your body for taking the special tasks and challenges of this phase of your life. Ask God to open you to the powers and delights of this special phase, as well as the special problems. Let your whole body, just as it is now, be held closely in God's nearness and love, as one who is precious to God and valued by God.

Rest in this strong love, breathing gently. When ready, conclude your prayer.

Listening to Our Bodies
in Prayer

It was my twenty-first birthday. I was sitting by the window of an old, run-down boarding house and hotel in western Wyoming. A thunderstorm was approaching, rumbling and flashing over the mountains. I was two thousand miles from my family, seventy miles from the nearest railroad and doctor, and I was convinced that I was having an attack of appendicitis!

This was my first job, my first time so far away from home. I had been invited by my denomination's board of home missions to spend the summer as a student pastor to the small Congregational church in this small western town, which had no permanent pastor. I was thrilled to have my first pastorate. I felt strong, in charge, inspired, and it was the first day of my work. But now I was having appendicitis. It began that afternoon when I got off the bus in this town full of strangers!

To be sure, I had had similar symptoms before which I had always checked out medically, and nothing was ever wrong. But this was *it*! So I sat by the window wondering what to do. I was surrounded by strangers, I had no car, and the doctor was seventy miles away!

I heard a soft knock at the door. There stood an old man, the only other resident at the little boarding house. Earlier at supper, he had told me exciting tales of his adventurous, rather disreputable life in the Wyoming wilderness sixty years earlier. As I stood at the door and stared at him appalled, he pulled a package of chewing gum out of his shabby coat pocket and handed it to me.

"Young lady, I noticed you looked sort of lonely at supper. Here's some gum. It will keep you from taking to the booze!"

I took the gum, thanked him, closed the door, and sat down on the bed, holding the little package. The incredible kindness of the most unlikely people! I didn't know whether to laugh or cry. All of a sudden I noticed that my "appendicitis" had vanished away!

Since that time, I have observed that I get exactly the same symptoms when I am anxious about something that I don't want to admit. Had I been a little bit wiser, I would have asked my body: "Is it really my appendix, or is there something else you are trying to tell me?"

If I had done so, my body might have communicated to me: "You are very young, and you are lonely and scared. Yes, I know that you are feeling happy and excited, but at the same time you are scared that something is going to happen to you or that you'll mess up your first big job."

Undoubtedly I would have protested: "Nonsense. I feel perfectly calm. Besides, ministers aren't *supposed* to feel scared. Ministers are supposed to trust God and feel brave and serene! Besides, what would my congregation think if they knew I was scared?"

If I had gone on listening, my body, so much more in touch with my real feelings than was my conscious self, would have signaled back: "I don't care what you think ministers are *supposed* to feel. You *are* scared! Do you really think God doesn't know all about how you feel?

God wants you to face your fear and let yourself be comforted."

But I was not wise enough to listen to my body at that time, so God sent me the kind old man with his chewing gum, instead. God has so much more compassion toward our real feelings than we do. God encounters our hurting and hurtful feelings *not* as tumors to be cut out or poison gases to be suppressed, but as wounded children to be embraced and healed. Trying to build a life of spiritual disciplines on unfaced, unhealed wounds is like building high-rise structures on an earthquake fault. If we don't let God touch and heal us in our deep hurting places, we become manipulative of ourselves and others. Our faithful bodies try ceaselessly to let us know what is really going on in our deep levels.

I do not mean that *every* bodily symptom is "all in the head." We do have to use our common sense. Not long ago, I began to have persistent, severe headaches every time I sat with my family in our living room in the evening. In vain, I tried all kinds of emotional analysis on myself. Finally someone suggested that I might be allergic to the oil in a romantic little lamp we had recently started using. We removed the oil lamp, and presto! No more headache! We do live in a world in which there are allergies, appendicitis, bacteria, viruses, earthquakes, accidents, storms, and pollution. We do carry genetic problems in our bodies in addition to the wounds and burdens of our communities. In a later chapter I will suggest ways of encountering these very real problems within a loving relationship with our bodies.

A recurring bodily symptom which seems, with all the best medical detective work, to have no organic or environmental cause, *might* be the "angel," the messenger within our bodies calling some unfaced stress to our attention. The body is not a minor but a *major* prophet!

In a recent workshop, some of us in the group began to ponder and share various ways by which our bodies signal to us.

"I get this pain between my shoulders," one woman volunteered. Several people nodded.

"With me, it's the lower back," said a man.

"Or the pit of my stomach," someone else shared. "Sometimes I twist my ankle and fall without reason."

Other people mentioned a squeezing feeling in the head. One young man told us how he would drop things and how even his handwriting changed when he was experiencing unfaced emotional distress.

"I get blurry vision and laryngitis," a minister admitted.

"I get chilly," a student told us. "My hands turn as cold as dead fish on an ice slab!"

Each of us there had our special "signals" that for years seemed to have no medical cause, but that *always* were related to unhealed stress. Usually we grimly endured them, swallowed pills, or just resigned ourselves to our "weak points." But what if they are not our weak points at all, but rather our *strong* points? These bodily parts are not only doing their own usual work, but they also have the thankless task of signaling messages to the whole self.

What deepening growth and understanding would we experience if we looked on these vulnerable areas no longer as exasperating enemies, but as strong friends who are trying to tell us something important? One thinks of that powerful verse in the "The stone which the builders rejected has become the chief cornerstone" (Psalm 118:22, NEB).

Sometimes the signals given us are not specific, localized symptoms at all. Sometimes we feel a heavy inertia, more pervasive than mere fatigue. All too quickly we condemn ourselves as "lazy," which is neither helpful nor responsive to the body's signal. Rather than merely labelling ourselves, we might ask our bodies *why* we feel this dragging inertia. If we listen, we might begin to discover that we have over-strained ourselves in some way or that we are inwardly resisting someone else's domination or other people's plans projected on us. Possibly our "inner judge," the part within us that loves to condemn and punish ourselves, may be supressing some important needs and energies. Our so-called laziness may be a valid protest!

Often the only signal we experience may be a *lack* of sensory feeling or a pervasive tension in the muscles as if we were covered in armor.

> Many of us discover in adult life that we feel less than whole, that the "feeling" part of us has been buried under all kinds of pressure and preoccupations. . . . A sense of self is not only a mental experience. We experience thoughts and emotions on a bodily level as well. . . . Parts of the self are expressed in the body as chronic muscular tensions. . . . For every individual pattern of muscular contraction, there is a corresponding repressed emotional state without which such tension would not exist. Contraction of muscles . . . creates a feeling of physical power and control over various sensations and emotions. "Armoring" of the body thus blocks primal pain.[3]

There are many sources of possible stress that our bodies signal to us.

We often have unrealistic expectations of ourselves, feeling that we ought to be always cheerful, loving, energetic. Often we feel that we are never quite measuring up to God's, others', or our own expectations for ourselves. We feel that it is alright for others to be cross, tired, grieving, and to have limits, but not for us. We use words like *ought* and *should* a great deal about ourselves. We find it hard to say no. It is hard to learn to receive nurture, to share our feelings, and to claim space and time for ourselves.

Other sources of stress are the many unhealed wounds and memories we have within us. Too often we refuse to give ourselves time to grieve or face the anger we feel after loss, trauma, injustice. Too often we hurry past our inner hurts trying to "forgive and forget." We tend to ignore the difference between the sin and the inner wound.

Our tendency to pick up the wrong "cross" provides another great cause of inner stress. We think that God requires us to pick up and carry every task that others will not do. But we can discern our true "cross," God's own guidance for us, by the joy and renewed energy we feel along with pain and sacrifice in our chosen tasks.

Stress can often reflect a deep repression of our inner powers and gifts. As we are inwardly healed, our deep, unique powers begin to wake from sleep, and often we fear and resist them.

Ignoring our seasons of the spirit can also be a source of stress. There are times when it feels natural to be active and out-flowing, and there are times when it feels natural to be more indwelling and contemplative. If we consistently expect the same level of spiritual, emotional, and physical activity of ourselves, we are headed for trouble.

Sometimes we might feel drained by other people around us. We might feel cold, tired, dizzy, anxious, or irritable during or after certain encounters with others, especially if we feel that these others have become emotionally dependent upon us. Often our bodies reflect and carry this pain of others.

Sometimes even our prayer life itself becomes a source of stress if it has become a rigid set of rules rather than a free relationship with God. Prayer can rapidly become a burden if we do not let God begin with us exactly as we are or if we become inflexible in our timing and method.

These are some of the stresses our bodies try to signal. Of course, it is not only through stress symptoms that our bodies speak. Our bodies also signal joy and well-being. We need to listen also to and through peace, pleasure, delight. I don't mean just the pleasure of single bodily parts, such as the taste buds of the tongue when we eat a doughnut. Much more important is the reaction of the whole body. Some people feel a warm, pleasurable serenity flowing through their whole bodies when they are living wholistic, responsive lives. Others feel a delighted warmth in some central bodily area such as the solar plexus. Some feel a new exuberance, a new vitality. Still others feel a quiet, elastic efficiency and "meshing" of the bodily parts. These signs of content and gratitude from our bodies are as important as distress signs.

We also need to remember, however, that if we are in the habit of taking heavy amounts of stimulants, such as caffeine, or depressants, such as alcohol, it is difficult or even impossible to hear the signals of our bodies. A former alcoholic once told me that a whole new world of sensory, bodily communication and appreciation opened to him as he was healed of his addiction. Not only could he see a beautiful picture or flower, but now he could *feel* it!

Most of us need, occasionally, to take pills for the relief of headache or stomach distress. But even as we take them, we need to remember that it is not enough to send relief to the *symptom*. That symptom is telling us, in the only way it can, that there is something about ourselves, our habits, or our surroundings that we need to know. Before we send our "angel," our messenger, to sleep, let's listen to it!

This faithful, alert listening to our bodies is a holy and necessary part of our spirituality. And what incredible changes it can bring into our lives!

Suggested Meditation of Listening to Our Bodies

Behold, thou desirest truth in the inward being; therefore teach me wisdom in my secret heart.

—Psalm 51:6

In a comfortable position, claim the love and nearness of God surrounding you in whatever symbolic way is best for you. Give thanks in the beautiful words of an old prayer that God is "closer than breathing, nearer than hands and feet."

Turn your attention to your body and start listening. Is there a sense of peace and well-being? If so, give thanks. Try to discern the reasons for this feeling.

Let your attention move gently through your whole body, and observe if there is any discomfort or tension, no matter how small.

Touch the uncomfortable bodily part. If you cannot touch it with your hand, touch it with attentive, loving thought. Thank this messenger for its important work of signaling. Ask if it is trying to tell you something important about your way of life or some unfaced need or hurt.

Take a while to listen. You may be quickly in touch

with some imbalance or some pressuring, draining aspect of your life. There may rise in your thoughts an old or recent memory that needs healing. You may feel a desire to weep. You may need to feel and express anger or hurt. Do not feel guilty about this. This is part of our human praying. Stay with this anger or hurt as long as you need. Visualize Jesus lifting and embracing this feeling like a hurt child.

You may not be able to locate or identify any special source of stress or hurt. Do not try to push or force the awareness. Just thank your body for its signals and ask God for guidance into the awareness of the stress. Breathe gently, lean on God's strength, and give thanks that your body speaks to you. When ready, conclude your listening prayer.

• 4 •

New Ways of Praying for Ourselves

It is not easy to learn to listen to our bodies. Some of us find it even harder to *pray* for our bodies! Why is it so hard to pray for ourselves? Do we feel selfish? Embarrassed? Out of control? Do we want to be the givers rather than the receivers?

Peter certainly felt that way at the last supper in the upper room, when Jesus knelt before him to wash his feet (John 13:5-8). Peter was startled and protesting. Any one of us would probably have felt the same. But Jesus told him both firmly and lovingly that learning to receive is as much a part of belonging as learning to give.

Peter had learned something by the time Jesus, now resurrected, met him and the other disciples on the beach and cooked and served them breakfast (John 21). Peter let himself be lovingly served, fed, and warmed. Only then did Jesus challenge Peter to go and feed the hungry of the world. We cannot be shepherds who guide and give until we have at least begun also to be sheep who follow and receive.

How can we learn to pray for our needs which our bodies signal to us? The first, deepest foundation of this prayer is the limitless love of God. We do not need to explain anything to God. We do not need to beg or to earn anything. We do not need to say "hear our prayer," because God has heard our need before we ever spoke it. Indeed, our praying is a response to God already speaking within our hearts!

We do not need to beg God to have mercy on us, because we have already been told that God is love. From before the beginning of time, God has had mercy on us and longed for our response. These forms of prayer are, indeed, ancient liturgical phrases, still widely used in our liturgies as well as in our personal prayers. The problem with them, however, is that they imply that it is *God* who will change when we pray. This implication can arouse a deep inner fear that a God who has asked to hear us or to have mercy *might*, after all, be sometimes deaf or merciless. The more we repeat these prayers, the deeper our fear might go. We do not need to search for God, because it is God who forever searches for *us*. It is God who says: "Behold, I stand at the door and knock; if any one hears my voice and opens the door, I will come in" (Rev. 3:20).

Ron DelBene helps us in his excellent book, *The Breath Of Life*.

> Unfortunately, many people view the will of God as rather like a ten-ton elephant hanging overhead, ready to fall on them. . . . Actually the word which we translate into English as *will* comes from both a Hebrew and a Greek word which mean "yearning." It is that yearning which lovers have for one another. Not a yearning of the mind alone or of the heart alone but of the *whole being*. A yearning which we feel is only a glimmering of the depth of the yearning of God for us.[4]

Or as Julian of Norwich expressed it with poignant power in three separate writings six hundred years ago:

Prayer and Our Bodies

God is thirsty for everyone.
This thirst has already drawn
the Holy to Joy
and the living
are ever being drawn and drunk.
And yet
God still thirsts and longs.

In God is endless friendship,
space, life and being.

God feels great delight
to be our Father
and God feels great delight
to be our Mother
and God feels great delight
to be our true Spouse.[5]

Of course, we don't always *feel* the actual presence of
this love. But if we consent to this love and claim it, its
actuality becomes the radical healing of our whole lives
and the power of our praying.

Another vital foundation of our praying is the realization that prayer does not merely inspire us to action but
is action. A generation ago I heard an English spiritual
leader, Gerald Heard, say that the person who prays is
channeling new, healing life into the world the same
way a living plant breathes oxygen into the atmosphere.
When I heard that, my whole approach to prayer began
to change. Any form of deep prayer is a great gift to the
world, for every time we pray in depth, the world
around us and the world within us begin to change. We
have the wrong word for a group gathering for a day of
prayer: far from being a "retreat," it is an "advance"!

A third essential foundation to prayer is our understanding that God wants us to begin exactly where we are and exactly the way we feel. We do not need to go through a prescribed ritual or a special set of words to approach God. Words are not important at all. God would rather hear us express our feelings and our problems through our own stumbling but honest thoughts than to use the words of the holiest saint on earth. We do not need to get up early in the morning to pray. Morning is no more sacred than afternoon or night. God is equally present in them all, and God wants us to enter into prayer with the same naturalness and spontaneity with which we would embrace and talk with our most beloved friend.

We begin to learn that prayer is meant to be releasing, neither diagnostic nor prescriptive. We cannot discern the true roots and depth of either our or anyone else's problems. Much less can we prescribe what answers are needed and just how and at what level they should come and begin.

For the Christian, prayer releases the whole problem into the healing hands, the healing light of Christ. Then, like expanding yeast within a loaf of bread, the light expanding in the darkness, the breath of life filling and reviving the lifeless body, the healing transformation begins its holy work at depths far below our conscious awareness.

Because of this, we may not immediately see the changes taking place. When we do finally see them, we find with surprise that they are often manifested in areas that seem (at first) unrelated to the problem.

Bryant, a middle aged man, asked a few loving friends to join him in prayer for the problem of his heavy smoking. He wanted to stop but seemed unable to, even though he had tried many different methods.

Rather than concentrating on the smoking habit

alone, Bryant's prayer group visualized Bryant's *whole* body released to the healing of Jesus Christ. Some of them visualized Jesus touching Bryant with healing hands, healing him totally emotionally and physically. Others visualized God's healing light flowing through Bryant's whole body. Others (who were not comfortable with visualization in prayer) just thought of him lovingly for a few minutes every day and inwardly said a few words claiming for him the whole healing power of Jesus Christ. But no matter what the method, they all agreed to focus on Bryant and his whole self—not the smoking.

For a few weeks, the smoking continued. Then Bryant noticed that he was beginning to calm down in many high stress situations. He noticed an increasingly relaxed response to ringing telephones, heavy traffic, delayed mail, long committee meetings. He began to look at people's faces, to look at animals, trees, the birds, the clouds. He began to smile more, to cry sometimes, to breathe more deeply and slowly. As the inner peacefulness and sense of nurture grew, Bryant felt the lessening of the compulsion to smoke. The compulsion began to feel less necessary because he was now receiving sustenance and stimulation from many sources. At this point, he tried some of the suggested methods again to stop smoking completely. Now, at last, they began to work for him.

The physical symptom of smoking had far deeper roots in Bryant's life than he had at first realized. Had he and the group concentrated only on the smoking problem, he might indeed have stopped the habit, because the power of thought is strong, but some other compulsive habit might well have taken its place until the deeper inner need and restlessness was healed.

Does this mean that we should never pray specifically

for a physical problem or habit? Certainly we should listen to the problem, look on the ingrained habit as a signal of stress and need, and send encouraging thoughts to the body as it works for health. But we need to remember that what appears to be one problem usually turns out to be a problem of the whole life, and that its consequences are borne by the whole body, even though the problem itself may be manifested in one area. So, though we focus lovingly and creatively on some special part, we should also daily release the whole self into the healing hands of Christ.

As we release those problems that are signaled to us by our bodies into the healing of Christ, we become aware of an astounding possibility. Just as our weak, vulnerable bodily areas might instead be our strong, "messenger" areas, so likewise the greatest stress points and problem spots of our whole lives might be the source of our greatest empowered giftedness!

That very sensitivity that made us vulnerable and anxious is what, when healed, makes us imaginatively and empathetically close to others.

That very power that makes us manipulative and aggressive may be the same power which, when healed, enables us to plan, organize, and create.

The inertia that blocks us now, when healed, may become the powerful power to discern, choose, and focus in integrity.

The God we see through Jesus Christ is not interested in destroying any part of us, but instead longs to heal and bring to creative fulfillment every one of our energies and powers.

A friend of mine, Phyllis Magal from Maryland, an artist and a graduate from a theological school, is experienced in spiritual growing through body work. Through her hands, she can often feel where the energy flow through someone else's whole body is impacted and congested. When she puts her sensitive hands near the lower back of someone who is having back pain, she usually senses that the bodily energy is not flowing freely. It feels congested there. She suggests that the person visualize bodily inner energy flowing like a river of light through the whole body, especially down the back and the legs, and from there into the ground. She has found that this can often relieve some of the pain.

I once heard her thoughtfully ponder if possibly a person's surplus fat might also be regarded as congested energy, impacted creativity. This is, of course, still very theoretical, but it might be helpful to visualize the energy of the full and heavy bodily parts flowing like a river of light into other bodily parts to help them in their work. Along with healthful eating and exercise, might this also help with our use of energy, which might have contributed to the weight problem in the first place?

This opens many exciting possibilities about our deep problems which, up to now, may have just made us despair and hate ourselves. For example, might the mess, clutter, and disorganization in which so many of us live and struggle, also be signs of enriched powers *in reverse*? When we look at our desks covered with unanswered letters, when we can't open our bureau drawers because the objects within have begun to flow down the back, when we arrive late and breathless for appointments and forget to return phone calls and cannot find or finish anything, yes, we *do* have a problem. And yes, we may need counseling. But instead of hating our chaos, we can learn to look on it as a sign of life and hope. Our surrounding clutter may be signaling to us, just as our bodies do: "You are a person of power and potential creativity. But your powers are blocked and congested. Your unreleased gifts and energy are creating widening circles of disorder around you." Listen to your problem; dialogue with it as if it were a person with a face. Is it telling you about a hidden, buried gift? Let in God's light and air to bring forth and release this creative gift.

Sometimes we are blocked in this release by unfaced, unhealed, inner wounds. Some of them are wounds that may have lived through generations. A young man once told me that his great-grandmother had been separated from her parents as a little girl and sent hundreds of miles away to a boarding school. The school had high hygenic and scholastic standards, but almost no loving warmth. The girl was not allowed to keep her stuffed animals because they were considered unsanitary. Nobody hugged or cuddled her. There was almost no warm, human contact for her anywhere during those formative years. When she cried or was angry, she was not punished, but she was coldly isolated until she "saw reason." She became a woman who was not able to express warm or angry feelings of any kind. The pain of this and the defensive response to that pain were still experienced in the family to the fourth generation.

Sometimes the wound that blocks us is a personal trauma in our own lives. Many of us still carry around hurting memories of our earliest days. Humiliation and fear experienced by a tiny child can be a lifelong burden. We may no longer even remember what caused our hurt originally, but our bodies remember and signal the unhealed pain to us with bewildering symptoms and muscular tension.

Susan Griffin explains the possible meaning of some of our bodily responses:

It is extremely difficult, perhaps next to impossible, to experience any sensation without an emotion. Memory attached itself to smell, to touch, to color. . . . The body holds memories of feelings from the past. To be touched, to move, to breathe, all these experiences of the body bring intense feelings to consciousness. A woman is touched on a certain place on her back, and she remembers an old grief from her childhood. . . . After moving and breathing, sinking deeper in the knowledge of his body, a man begins to weep . . . as he relives an incident from his youth. In his analytical work, Wilhelm Reich found that the emotional amnesias, called "blocks," and muscular tensions were . . . "functionally identical."

Nothing brings the soul to feel so much as physical sensation, for emotions live in the body; we know a whole physical language of emotion.[6]

Many of us have already experienced this truth of physical recall of our former hurts and joys. It is not always a specific memory that surfaces when we listen to our body's signals. Sometimes mingled and unfocused feelings of sadness, happiness, pain, anxiety, anger, come to our attention. Sometimes we may just wish to weep without knowing why.

Nothing within us, however, is wasted or cast aside within God's love. Our problems and pretenses are not onionskins to be peeled off. Our masks are not true masks at all. They are the very lineaments of our fear and woundedness. God will not tear off our masks, nor should we tear them off of ourselves or one another. *They are part of us, these masks—our frightened part.* As such, they will be lovingly encountered by God and healed. Even our closed doors are in themselves the very presence of our frozen pain. God encounters these shut doors with infinite compassion, knowing we are pathetically revealing our vulnerability. Every tense muscle, every defensive withdrawal is a beloved and wounded child who is to be embraced and restored to life and released to empowerment.

Jesus said, "The kingdom of heaven is like leaven [yeast] which a woman took and hid in three measures of meal, till it was all leavened" (Matt. 13:33). In this powerful analogy of the inexorable, radical change that begins within us at the deepest levels as we welcome God's healing, we approach our prayer for all the needs our bodies signal to us.

Suggested Prayer for the Body and the Wounds of Memory

O God, thou art my God, . . . my soul thirsts for thee; my flesh faints for thee, as in a dry and weary land where no water is. . . . My soul clings to thee; thy right hand upholds me.

—Psalm 63:1, 8

Thus says the Lord who made you, who formed you from the womb and will help you: Fear not. . . . For I will pour water on the thirsty land, and streams on the dry ground.

—Isaiah 44:2-3

In a restful posture, breathe gently and slowly. Picture God's love rising like a healing spring of water, a river of light from the very center of the earth. Picture it flowing slowly into your feet and legs, and then, with each slow, gentle breath, rising higher into the body: up through the abdomen, the back, the fingers, the arms, the chest, the shoulders, the neck, into your facial muscles (especially the eyes and jaw), into the whole head area, then flowing from the head like a fountain and down around the outside of the body. Your whole body is filled and covered with the warm, healing river of light.

Relax into this warm, flowing light. Think of every cell of your body now washed and refreshed. Let the healing waters move to any parts of your body that are in discomfort or tension. As they are bathed in God's waters, listen to their signals. What are they trying to tell you? Is some unhealed hurt being brought to your attention?

If ready and willing, picture yourself rising from the healing waters and walking with Jesus to the memory of that hurt. If you do not wish yet to face it, do not push yourself, but ask Christ to go ahead of you to fill and "soak" that place of pain until you are ready to encounter it.

If you wish to face it with Christ, go to that place and sit with Christ (in whatever symbolic form Christ comes to you) in that place of memory. Let yourself feel your feeling as long and deeply as necessary. Don't try to produce pious emotions. Let yourself grieve, weep, experience anger or fear. You are not alone. This is a safe place, as you lean on God's love and stay fully with your feeling.

This may be enough for today or for several days. You may want to come back to this place several times before the next step. But if ready, give consent that Christ calls to those other people involved with your memory of pain. In your imagination visualize these people coming through the door, coming as the wounded little boys or girls they are inwardly.

Do not force yourself to love or touch them if you are not ready. Trust the meditation and let the other person's inner child act in whatever way seems spontaneous. They may weep with their own pain or show their needs to be perfect or important or to experience love and acceptance. Probably in this prayer you are encountering their own pain and fear, which you had never seen before.

Picture the Christ interacting with you both in some healing way. Observe what seems to happen, remembering you are perfectly safe. *If at any point you wish to stop this form of picturing prayer, feel free to do so.* When ready, walk back with Christ to the present moment, rest in love, relaxing your body, perhaps entering again the healing waters. When ready, conclude the prayer.

––––––––––––

You may wish to repeat the symbolic washing of your body in God's waters every day. You may need to return to specific memories once or several times. Every time it is different. Eventually, you will know when it is no longer necessary to go back to a certain memory. There will be a sense of having completed the work, and a kind of closure will take place.

Suggested Prayer for the Healing of Your Unnamed Inner Pain

Your sun shall no more go down, nor your moon withdraw itself; for the Lord will be your everlasting light, and your days of mourning shall be ended.

—Isaiah 60:20

Jesus returned in the power of the Spirit. . . . And he stood up to read: . . . "The Spirit of the Lord is upon me. . . . He has sent me to proclaim release to the captives and recovering of sight to the blind, to set at liberty those who are oppressed."

—Luke 4:14, 16, 18

Relax your body, and take a few minutes for nurturing prayer. Claim Christ's promised presence and let the living Christ come to you in whatever way is best for you.

Give thanks that the living Christ is with you and ready to walk with you to the entrance of your unknown, subconscious self where dwell so many hurts and unawakened gifts.

Your symbolic expression of this entrance may look like a door, a cave, a tunnel, a well, an adjoining room. In your own words, give consent that Christ goes with full healing power into your subconscious self. The love of God has always dwelt there, but now you give consent for the full *healing* to become affective.

Your conscious self should not attempt to go into those depths. There is nothing there that can harm us, but we are not always ready to encounter fully our buried hurts and powers. God is merciful and brings us to the encounter only when we are ready and able.

See Christ going through the entrance, into the deep places. There lie the wounded children so far down that we barely knew of their presence. We may not have heard their crying until our bodies signaled to us their presence. Give thanks that the merciful hands of healing are laid upon everyone of these little ones. See yourself standing by the entrance, giving thanks that all are being touched and that the transformation has begun. We may not yet see or feel this, but the change has begun at the very center, like the yeast working in the loaf.

When it seems the right time, see the Christ coming back through the entrance, perhaps bringing something or someone to show us. Welcome it in whatever way seems natural and spontaneous.

Now see the Christ putting under protection this

entrance to your deepest self. Only that which comes in the love of God may ever enter there.

Now rest quietly in the love of God and the presence of the Christ, breathing the nurture, and giving thanks. When ready, conclude the meditation.

———————

If you find that visualizing is not comfortable or natural for you, it is enough to enter into any form of relaxed, nurturing prayer. In whatever words or thoughts are best for you, simply give consent that God through Christ is healing and transforming your deep, unknown inner self. Give thanks in your own way and your own words.

When we pray for the healing of this very core of our self, it seems to affect our bodies more profoundly than almost any other kind of prayer. This is because our bodies are always in touch with our subconscious feelings. As the inner wounds are healed and the inner gifts begin to be released, we will begin to notice many changes of our bodily symptoms, signals, and responses. Often the nature of our dreams will also begin to change, some of our phobias will be affected, and many of our relationships will begin to heal. For by thus praying, we are consenting not only to the *love* of God which is always with us, but the full *healing power* of God. And the divine "yeast" begins its radical work. In *The Living Bible's* paraphrase of Ephesians 3:20-21, we see a beautiful expression of God's vitality within us.

> Now glory be to God who by his mighty power at work within us is able to do far more than we would ever dare to ask or even dream of—infinitely beyond our highest prayers, desires, thoughts, or hopes.

5

Letting
Our Bodies
Pray

Coming into my room, tired after a full day of teaching and counseling, I saw through the window a small bird splashing in the rain-filled gutter of the porch roof. Its little body ecstatically cleansed itself as it flapped its wings and ruffled its dusty feathers. The moment was one of those tiny sabbaths which are scattered through our days. Almost without thinking about it, I moved to the basin and began to wash *my* face and hands. Suddenly and eagerly my body claimed this act of washing as a cleansing and release from the tasks and problems of the day.

"Is my body really teaching me to pray?" I wondered. It was an exciting thought. I had learned (with difficulty) to pray for my body, but letting my body take the lead and show me new ways of praying was a sudden, new possibility.

If our bodies signal stress to us, communicate inner problems, and become increasingly our true partners in our emotional and spiritual living, why shouldn't they also signal to us spontaneous ways of praying? Are there deep and beautiful ways of encountering God's nearness which we have not experienced, simply because we have not allowed our bodies to be full spiritual partners?

I began to observe my body in some of its most natural and spontaneous acts. Slowly I began to realize that when our bodies are not interfered with by artificial constraints and stimulants, their every act is meant to be a sacramental way of receiving nurture from God. The simple yet satisfying yawning and stretching when we awake can be an act of prayer if we so choose. The word *inspiration* actually refers to the act of breathing. Just as God breathed the breath of life into the first living being, so our deep, instinctive taking of breath is receiving again the gift of life from God for each moment. Stretching fully flexes the muscles, stimulates the circulation, and is another way by which the body breathes and thus prays. Tasting and eating can become the body's way of receiving God's nurture through the gifts of the earth. All the five senses can become ways of profound receiving and giving. I have sometimes thought that certain forms of physical addiction might result from sensory starvation rather than from over-sensuousness.

We were intended to receive God's full energizing nurture through all five senses. If we try to receive life's energy only through one or two senses, we may become over-dependent on those channels. If we overeat, over-drink, depend on constant sexual encounters, need to talk constantly or be always surrounded by loud music, we need not only to be released from our addictions but also to *expand* our sensory awareness through other ways.

If we overeat, for example, depending on the com- *eating* fort of food as the only energy giver and the only source of comforting nurture, it would be helpful to listen quietly to our bodies for a few minutes rather than to head automatically for the kitchen. Our bodies can then signal to us how we are really feeling and suggest other ways by which we can receive comfort and energy.

Perhaps we would find it helpful to dance and stretch in our rooms instead, letting our bodies express what we feel and want and need. We can get in touch with many buried feelings this way. Klarise Davis, of the Loretto Community in Albany, California, once told me, "Anger causes toxins to form in the large muscles of the body. In order to release these toxins, use them in exercise, releasing also the stored anger."

Grieving, hurt, and loneliness can often be reached and expressed in this same way. Sometimes we will want to use our whole body to express the feeling; sometimes it will be enough just to let the hands, feet, or head move. At other times, just listening to music and letting it fill us will meet and feed our hunger.

We can also receive nourishment for our inner hungers and needs by visualizing light rising from the very center of the earth and then, either standing or sitting, drawing it up with our hands as if pulling a warm garment of light over our whole body. Or we can stretch up and out with our hands and arms as if receiving energizing light coming from above and around us. This stretching should not be jerky or abrupt, but should be gentle, thoughtful, flowing. I was very helped by a suggestion from Mary Anne Finch, codirector of the Center of Growth and Wholeness in Oakland, California, about the prayerful stretch: "Be still and see the posture in your mind. Then slowly move into it. Hold the posture, then slowly move out of it. Pause, and allow your body to acknowledge the benefits of the stretch."

What I am suggesting here is not the same boring maxim, "Cut out the overeating and exercise instead." That misses the point and puts us right back into the same desperate war between our willpower and our unencountered hungers. Rather, I am suggesting a new understanding of *both* eating and exercise (as well as of all our other physical actions) as ways of receiving God's loving grace. If we find we have depended too much on one way only, God invites us to expand our ways of receiving in many other ways.

If body movement is not possible or appropriate at the moment, our whole selves can also be reenergized by looking at some loved color in a rock, a flower, a fabric, a picture. Color is astonishingly energizing. If we take a few moments, we will often feel drawn to some special color which will "feed" us at that moment. I remember during some weeks when I was depleted after the flu, I felt the need to look often at a certain shade of red; to touch it, wear it. It seemed to warm and strengthen me. At another time, I kept dreaming of a luminous shade of blue and finally realized that my deep self was trying to signal me that this special color was important for me at that time. Historians tell us that the walls of the great cathedrals of the middle ages were not whitewashed as so many of them are now, but were painted with frescoes of rich colors. And, of course, the stained glass windows were not only showing the Bible stories to those who could not read but were also feeding with radiant color the bodies and souls of those who lived bleak, exhausting lives outside those church walls. Whether or not the builders and craftsmen realized this, human needs were being fed on many levels.

The receiving of energy through sensory channels need not be through sight alone. We can let water run over our hands, giving its special gift. We can hold a flower to smell or a stone or crystal to touch. We can gently massage the hands, arms, neck, face, feet. Our loving touch on our own bodies is healing and comforting. When we eat, we can do it slowly, deliberately, gratefully, noticing the taste, texture, and fragrance of the food, knowing that every bite is a loving gift of God's nearness.

We can go outdoors and put our hands on a living shrub, receiving the vibratory energy from that living being. We can open our palms and lift our faces to the sunlight and air, taking nurture from that primal source. We can lie down on the ground, letting the strong earth hold our full weight like a father, mother, or trusted friend.

Try taking a "parable walk," in which you set out with no special agenda, asking God to show you something that will be meaningful, relevant to your problems and feelings. Whenever I take a parable walk or suggest it to members of a retreat, there is always something observed or experienced that is helpful. It is not usually something sensational. Other people may have noticed nothing, but it seems significant for your life. It might be something about a cloud, a tree, a door. It may be the way a tree is shaped, what an ant is doing, or how a bird is sounding. It might be someone's face, the way the breeze feels, or the way a dog is barking. But there will be something God wanted you to encounter. Perhaps it will evoke a memory whose time for healing has come. It may offer guidance for an unsolved problem. It may give you the inner nurture you need. You may be comforted or become aware of a new insight. You may be enabled to laugh, to weep, to love, or to release.

When receiving God's gifts and nurture through the senses, it is essential to be deliberate, aware, focusing upon each event, receptive to each sensory experience in its uniqueness. This is the very opposite of greed and lust, which are usually based upon unhealed wounds, anxiousness, fear of deprivation, and the resulting habits of grasping rather then receiving.

Expressing our needs and feelings and receiving God's nurture can be experienced alone or in the company of a trusted group. Many spiritual leaders are developing and sharing ways by which spiritual and emotional growth can be enhanced through bodily expression. A warning, however, is appropriate here. Some leaders are insufficiently aware of the reserves and shyness of many participants, especially beginners. Some leaders are tempted to rush participants too quickly into full bodily expression and group interaction before they are fully ready. Often embarrassed and resentful, members will drop out, sadly assuming that prayer through body work is not for them. Or, even worse, they will remain, obeying the leader, complying with group expectations, trying to ignore or silence their inner protests.

The experience of prayer through the symbolic action of our bodies is extremely powerful. Here, as in all areas of spiritual/emotional growth and expression, spiritual guidance must not become spiritual assault. The discerning leader will realize that everyone has his or her own timing and will respect these timings. A loving leader will know that most people carry unhealed wounds and defenses and that many people are acutely uneasy and uncomfortable with their own physical selves and those of others. Many are hesitant and even frightened of their own sleeping bodily and emotional powers. There are also those who are just private people who need time and a growing trust to reveal themselves.

A friend told me recently that she had been to a body workshop in which the leader during the very first hour of the first day had the participants scratching and rubbing each other's backs; getting on the floor to enact the animals that had been assigned to them; and dancing in a circle, bodily shaking out all the inner hurts, tensions, and reserves! Some of the participants loved it. But others, probably those who needed most to learn a new relationship with their bodies, felt violated. They never returned.

Very different is the approach of another leader I know. This retreat leader approaches with gentleness the hesitancies and defenses of beginning participants. In introducing people to the bodily dimensions of prayer, she asks group members to close their eyes (which she does too), and then encourages them to allow their bodies to express whatever seems natural in response to such words as *joy, fear, grieving, guilt, peace, praise, loneliness, love,* and others. In a context aimed at minimizing self-consciousness, yet supported by others engaged in the same exercise, each person works out his or her own timing, rhythm, and manner of physical expression.

This friend told me that at first group members often report feeling comfortable moving only the arms, head, and upper torso, but as trust in the group and comfort with their own physical response deepens, they are able to move toward full bodily expression of their feelings and attitudes before God.

In another exercise, she leads members in the Lord's Prayer, suggesting that at first they cross their arms and legs to see if such a posture affects their experience of the prayer. Then, she invites them to repeat the prayer while they kneel and open out their hands. In this way, they can observe for themselves how the whole personal response to God's love is deepened when the body is allowed to be a guide and partner in prayer rather than a hindrance to it.

58

In any kind of group interaction, permission should always be given to sit quietly, to pull back inwardly, not to participate. The more powerful the material with which we work, the more important it is to respect one another's freedom and to give (and claim) releasing permissions.

Recently I have seen a remarkable demonstration of body expression of the whole self. The leadership staff of a workshop for spiritual formation provided modelling clay and crayons and encouraged, but did not push, participants to use these materials to express their feelings and responses during the lectures, discussions, and guided meditations. Great works of art were not expected. No one was required to show his or her handwork. Through such creative motions of the hands, responding to inner impulses, many things can be expressed: excitement, hurt, fear, anger, defense, joy, longing, eagerness, bewilderment. Some participants might form a model of the inner wounded child within them. Others might shape a part of the body itself. In this way our bodies help us form a symbolic representation of our problem or feeling so that we can encounter it directly.

Sometimes when I suggest some forms of bodily prayer in a retreat or workshop, people are surprised. "You mean that touching a tree, taking a walk, lying on the grass, dancing, eating, stretching, playing with clay can be *prayer*?" one middle-aged man recently asked in bewilderment. "I never thought of those things as spiritual. Maybe prayer is easier than I thought."

Yes, prayer *is* easier than we thought. Prayer was always meant to be part of our everyday lives, part of our bodies, part of all our actions. It does not mean that we are to be solemn and unsmiling as we act sacramentally through our bodies. A sacrament, whether in the church or out of it, is meant to make us more fully human, not less. "The glory of God is the fully alive human being," Iranaeus said in the second century. Yes, we are to respond to the body's acts of worship with intentionality, awareness, deliberation, but also with pleasure and joy.

One of the holiest experiences I ever had was also one of the most bodily. My husband and I were invited to join a Jewish couple for their sabbath meal. The food was simple, lovingly prepared, and flavorful. Between courses, we celebrated one of the five senses. At one point, our hosts passed around a flower for us to contemplate, touch, and smell. At another point, a piece of fruit was passed from hand to hand, with each person experiencing the fruit. Later, we sang a short song, delighting in the melody and in each other's voices. This sensory awareness of God's gifts was woven into the act of eating. I had seldom sat at a table where there was so much joy, laughter, and closeness to one another along with the sense of the nearness of God and the holiness of God's gifts. Our bodies love to pray and rejoice and bring us closer to God, if only we let them!

Suggested Meditation for the Body's Breathing

[Jesus] breathed on them, and said to them, "Receive the Holy Spirit."

—John 20:22

Let everything that breathes praise the Lord!

—Psalm 150:6

Gently and lightly massage the hands, face, and neck. Claim with trust the presence of Jesus Christ, the incarnate love of God, always with you. Relax your body, and picture around you some light, color, water, breeze, or other symbol of God's energizing and enfolding presence.

Listen to any signals from the body of physical discomfort, pain, tension, unease. Focus on that part of your body, feeling it breathing in and out as if that part had its own separate breathing apparatus. Let that body part breathe slowly for several minutes. Visualize God's surrounding light or breath flowing in and out of that area.

When it feels right, move on to another area, letting that area breathe in and out. This is a powerful pain reliever. Now let your whole body breathe slowly, gently from the soles of the feet to the top of the head. Don't gasp or push it.

Now just sit quietly, leaning on the strength of God, letting God's life-giving breath flow in and out of your body. Give thanks, and when ready, open your eyes.

Suggested Meditation for the Body's Prayer and Worship

As a hart longs for flowing streams, so longs my soul for thee, O God. My soul thirsts for God, for the living God.
—Psalm 42:1-2

My heart and flesh sing for joy to the living God.
—Psalm 84:2

While silently or vocally repeating the Lord's Prayer and Twenty-third Psalm, some beloved hymn, or a prayer of your own composing, encourage your body to express what you are feeling. You may wish to move your whole body or just the hands, arms, head, or facial muscles. Don't imitate what others do nor enact what you think you should be feeling and doing. Just follow your body's guidance for your own genuine feelings. Let the motions be as relaxed, gentle, and flowing as possible.

If you would prefer, sit quietly with eyes closed and image your body moving or dancing in prayer in the presence of God. Visualize your body moving in thanksgiving, grieving, healing, petition, intercession. Let your gentle rhythmic breathing flow into the inner image of yourself moving in prayer.

Now visualize your body moving more and more deeply into the light and nearness of God in whatever way you are led.

Quietly rest and lean on God's strength. When ready, open your eyes and conclude the meditation.

6

Healed Empowerment
and Our Bodies

A group of us, exploring the power of prayer together, sat by the fire and shared some of our changing experiences and dreams.

"I had a strange dream last night," one of the older women told us. "I dreamed it was the night before my wedding, and I realized I was terribly frightened—frightened most of all of my bridegroom. He came in the room, and I told him how I felt. He understood, and we sat down quietly together. I laid my head on his knee and he stroked my hair, comforting me gently. My fear began to be healed."

This dream can have many interpretations, of course. Our friend who experienced the dream thought that its main meanings were of her fear of love and empowerment and of her need for that fear to be comforted and healed.

Do we rush and challenge ourselves and our powers too quickly in our Christian communities? Are we too demanding of a quick flowering of God's gifts within us? Most of us are still wounded, frightened people needing inner healing. Far too little attention is given to this healing in most of our church services, prayers, liturgies, and confessions. We still do not provide enough help to one another in discerning between sins and wounds. We still expect fruit to spring from wounded branches. Continually we forget Jesus' primary passion to heal and nurture and *then* to empower.

"But doesn't the healing often come *with* the use of our powers?" one retreat member asked. "If we sit licking our wounds all our lives and don't go out and use our gifts and make ourself do things, aren't we missing one of the main ways to be healed?"

This is true up to a point. I heard one wise teacher of psychology and religion say, "Christ meets us where we are, but does not leave us there." As we are encountered fully and lovingly, our healing deepens and our powers inevitably and inexorably begin to rise. If we try to force them to rise when we are still uncomforted and unhealed, we endanger ourselves. It is also true that if we do not use the gifts that come during our healing, we equally endanger ourselves. As a teenager, I was so desperately shy that I was reluctant to go to church lest someone should speak to me! After church one Sunday, one of the youth group leaders, a gentle young woman, came up with a friendly smile and said, "I badly need your help. The girl who was going to turn the piano book pages for me while I play the piano tonight at the meeting is sick. Could you please come tonight and turn the pages for me?"

Reluctantly, I agreed to do her this favor. After all, it wouldn't be *too* scary. It's not as if they asked me to speak, sing, or be conspicuous. So I turned the pages for her that night and agreed to come the following week to help set up chairs. Soon they got me out into the kitchen to help with the supper. I began to go to the group regularly, and never did they push me to do anything I wasn't ready to do. In two years, I agreed to become the worship leader. In three years, I agreed to serve as vice-president of the group. A year after that, I entered theological school to prepare for the ministry! I think back with such gratitude for that wise and loving group that gave me as much time as I needed for my inner healing, that gently encouraged (and never forced) me to use my new-born gifts as they arose.

God promises us that these gifts and powers *will* rise. God heals us, first, so that our suffering may be ended. But God also heals us so that we may enter fully into the creative passion of God's own power. God heals us so we may be co-workers on the frontier where creation meets chaos, pushing back the limits.

God comforts us, even as the bridegroom comforted the bride in my friend's dream. But we will not spend all eternity being stroked on the hair and comforted by God.

> They who wait for the Lord shall renew their strength,
> they shall mount up with wings like eagles,
> they shall run and not be weary,
> they shall walk and not faint.
>
> . . . .
>
> Then shall your light break forth like the dawn,
> and your healing shall spring up speedily;
> your righteousness shall go before you,
> the glory of the Lord shall be your rear guard.
> —Isaiah 40:31; 58:8

This is God's promise, that we will be summoned, called, married to the passion of creative love and un-dreamed of activity and involvement.

This can be a scary thought! How would the acorn feel if shown the full oak tree? How would the unborn baby feel if it could be shown the full-grown man or woman? How would I have felt that night as I shrink-ingly turned the pages of music if someone had suddenly said, "In five years you will be preaching sermons"? How would you feel if five years ago, or even one year ago, you had been shown what you are now enabled to do? John writes in his first letter: "Beloved, we are God's children now; it does not yet appear what we shall be, but we know that when he appears we shall be like him, for we shall see him as he is" (1 John 3:2). Does this verse sum up the foundation of both our healing and our empowering?

Part of our reluctance to release our powers comes from the knowledge that we will have to face new problems, that we will be changed. We will be vulnerable, and we will have to become assertive. We will love, suffer, laugh, and weep. Some of our relationships will deepen incredibly, but others will end because some friends are more comfortable with us in our old, unhealed, powerless state.

Perhaps we are afraid our powers will get out of control and fragment us and those around us. We have seen misuse of power. Can we trust our use of it, even as healed and healing persons? Might it be safer for everyone not to let it out at all?

Did Jesus feel this way at his baptism when the Holy Spirit empowered him? Did he feel this way when he went alone into the wilderness to face the meaning and use of his powers? Did he feel this way when his mother asked him to help with the failing wine supply at the wedding feast in Cana? Jesus knew that once he had revealed himself in this way, he could not go back. His decision to move into the full use of his powers within the immediacy of God was as significant as his decision three years later to enter Jerusalem at the Passover, knowing that the cross awaited him there. This decision at Cana was part of what we call the *Epiphany,* the revealing of the full empowered light within Jesus.

When James and John asked to enter into his powers (Mark 10:35-45), Jesus did not rebuke them. He asked them if they were ready to pay the price. Could they undergo his baptism and drink from his sacrificial cup? Empowerment is given not to control others, but to serve others. God is not a *bland* God! We are in a universe of storms, electricity, powers, and polarities. Healing does not render us passive and passionless. G. K. Chesterton wrote:

> Sometimes this pure gentleness and this pure fierceness met and justified their juncture; the paradox of all the prophets was fulfilled, . . . and the lion lay down with the lamb. But remember that this text is too lightly interpreted. It is constantly assured . . . that when the lion lies down with the lamb the lion becomes lamblike. But that is brutal annexation and imperialism on the part of the lamb. That is simply the lamb absorbing the lion instead of the lion eating the lamb. The real problem is— Can the lion lie down with the lamb and still retain his royal ferocity? *That* is the problem the Church attempted.[7]

The transformation by the Holy Spirit does not mean blandness. Rather it means poise, balance, justice, and charity between the passionate powers and energies. It means not a watering down of the strengths, but a healing of a marriage between the strengths!

Our bodies are often the first to signal the rising of our newly released inner energies and gifts. It is perhaps impossible to experience emotional or spiritual change without some corresponding bodily change. It is beautifully expressed by one of the great spiritual writers of the Middle Ages, Mechtild of Magdeburg:

Prayer and Our Bodies

As love grows and expands in the soul,
　　it rises eagerly to God
　　　　and overflows
　　　　　　towards the Glory
　　which bends towards it.

Then Love melts through the soul
　　　into the senses,
　　so that the body too might share in it,
for Love
　　is drawn
　　　　into all things.[8]

A new restlessness, poignancy, vigor is felt in the body that often involves a heightened sexual awareness, a new release through tears and laughter, a new awareness of anger as the justice of healing and compassion deepens, and a new-born pain of awakened concern for the suffering of those around us. There is also a new keen awareness of the healed, cleansed five senses as discussed in the previous chapter. Sometimes as we experience deepened healing and release, we become aware of the vibratory energy field around our bodies.

A new longing to be closer to others is one of the great signs of our healed and rising powers, as we gain the ability to feel both pain and joy as never before. We find ourselves hurting for others in a way previously unknown to us. It is harder to open the newspaper at the breakfast table and blandly read about wars, famine, earthquake, and accident. We notice the loneliness and grief in the faces of people we pass on the street. We hurt with the hurting of others and long to break down the dividing walls to share the griefs. It is not only our deepening humanity we are feeling with this pain, but also the pain and longing of God's own heart, the God we see through Jesus.

It is a temptation in this new empowerment of empathy to brush too quickly aside the limits and reserves of others. These reservations may be based on their unhealed hurts and fears or may be the result of their own personal timing of unfolding and response. Somewhere I read that if there was an eleventh commandment it would read, "Thou shalt not move thy neighbor's boundary stone."

We should always be careful to pray for inner guidance before we try to become channel for the healing of others. I have not always been thus careful. Twenty-three years ago, a very troubled young woman came to make her home with my family for a while. Confident and brash in my newly discovered enthusiasms for prayer, I announced to her one day that I would come to her room each morning, lay hands on her head, and pray for her complete healing. I didn't ask her. I *told* her! She didn't protest, but neither did she respond to the gesture with real consent. Completely insensitive to her freedom and her feelings, I went into her room each morning, knelt by her bed, layed hands on her head and prayed while she lay half-buried under the covers in silence. Needless to say, there was no observable change for the better in her emotional health, which puzzled me mightily at the time!

Our longings for intimacy, sharing, and healing closeness to others is indeed one of the transformed and transforming powers that rise within us as our healing deepens. We are not asked to repress the beautiful gifts of our enthusiasms, love, longing to heal. Rather, we are asked with equal passion to honor, cherish, and value the freedom and unique identity of other persons. This is the difference between the Holy Spirit and lesser spirits.

Another growing empowerment in our bodily feelings is the ability to express joy and praise. The longing to praise, rejoice, and take delight is not only a sign of healing, but also a mighty nurturing force for even deeper healing. The inability to celebrate God, others, and, yes, ourselves means that there is still something defended and unreleased within us.

The ability to receive the delight and praise of others can be even harder. We don't often think of how God longs to praise us! Yet the scriptures are full of this longing. There is a beautiful paraphrase of the famous old benediction in Numbers 6:24-25 to be found in *The Living Bible*: "May the Lord bless and protect you; may the Lord's face radiate with joy because of you." What a magnificent thought that we can give delight to God, rather than just arouse God's pity and compassion! I believe the warmth we feel through our whole selves, body and feelings, when we have dared to love, dared to give, dared to meet life with generous openness is the smile of God!

The gifts of tears and laughter are among the signs of empowered release. Tears do not necessarily mean sadness or depression. Tears can be a cleansing act of warm closeness to the life within and around us. Tears are often the opening and pouring forth of deep springs of inner life. Even when they do come from grief, the ability to grieve openly and freely is a bodily sign of trust and release.

Laughter, too, is a whole body response to God's life within us. As we are healed, our laughter is no longer the laughter of defense and mockery but the delighted sensory encounter with the unexpected, the incongruous, the ludicrous that is such an essential part of our humanness as it grows within God's own abundant life.

Some of the manifestations of our increasing bodily

Healed Empowerment and Our Bodies

and emotional empowerment may be disconcerting to us at first. For example, our sexual feelings often intensify as we are made more whole. Many think that sexuality will go away or at least become quiescent as we grow spiritually. On the contrary! As we abide more closely to the God who is the source of all creative energy, the God of the Incarnation, we begin to experience sexual energy in a new way, as a holy, inalienable, generative force.

Our sexuality is not merely a matter of romance, procreation, or specific sexual activity. It is not even solely a matter of relationship. Sooner of later, for most of us, our sexuality will probably be related to some or all of these, but in itself, it belongs to a more primal core within us. Sexual energy is energy from the source of creative life itself. It rises with such awesome power that every known culture in the world, no matter how primitive, has developed structures, limits, taboos, guidelines for the chaneling of this energy. It is part of the exultation, the fiery power and the passion of life. It is involved with our feelings about ourselves: our bodies, our inner powers, our wounds, the world around us. Perhaps most of all, our sexuality is our empowered response to our inner polarities: the contrasts, the opposites, the mingling of the nurturing and the assertive, the solitary and the relational, the quiescent and the active, the cooperative and the competitive, all living within us as part of our full humanness. We are all sexual beings, including those who are celibate or abstinent, for our creative polarized response to life within and around us is manifested in many ways through our body's vitality.

As explained in the introduction, it is not the purpose of this book to focus on ethical decisions. When and if, however, we choose to give direct expression to our sexuality, some guiding questions may be appropriate. These questions rise from the witness of this book that our bodies are our God-given companions for the deepening of our spiritual wholeness:

Am I hurting or harming anyone, or endangering anyone's health, including my own, by my sexual activity?

Am I violating any of my commitments, relationships, responsibilities? Am I breaking any promises?

Am I trying to grow into a faithful and committed relationship with my partner?

Does my sexual activity increase my power to love others with compassion and concern? Or is my use of sexuality an act of bargaining, submission, manipulation?

Am I able to carry God's love and presence with me into my sexual activity? Am I able to celebrate fully my form of sexual activity as a member of the Body of Christ?

Is my sexual activity a part of my deep, whole self, or a compartmentalized activity, cut off from the rest of the way I feel, think, and act?

Does my sexual activity make me feel healthier, more whole, increasing my honor of and delight in my own body?

Would it trouble me if my sexual activity were known by others whom I respect?

Of course, there are times when overt expression of our sexual energies would be inappropriate or damaging. How can we relate to our bodies and our feelings at these times, when we choose to say no to sexual activity?

We need not waste our feelings of sexual empowerment. Our bodies are offering us primal energy for our whole selves at such times. Sexual feeling does not come from our "lower selves." *None* of our bodily energies are low or unworthy. As Paul wrote to the church at Corinth: "Those parts of the body which we think less honorable we invest with the greater honor" (1 Cor. 12:23). How we choose to express the energy may be unworthy or destructive, but the radiant energy itself, the song of our sexuality, is often one of the first signs of new gifted vitality awakening within us.

We can speak inwardly to our sexual emotion: "I hear you gladly. You are a deep and wonderful part of me. You are signaling life and strength and offering me a great gift. At this time, in this situation, however, I choose not to give you *direct* expression; rather I ask you to send your powerful vitality to my whole self so that I can do my work with empowered love."

If this inner dialogue seems uncomfortable or contrived, try to locate the place in your body where this emotional energy seems to be centered, whether the heart, abdomen, or pelvic area, and then picture the energy flowing with radiant power like a river of light into all parts of your body. Especially let it flow to any bodily areas needing warmth and strength. Picture it flowing to your eyes, ears, or brain if you are walking, driving, reading, listening to music, or watching drama. Visualize it flowing to your brain, throat, and mouth when you are talking, teaching, or preaching, and then out to your group. If counseling, picture this river of light rising to your heart and flowing with warmth to the other person. Let it flow to your heart and hands if nursing, writing, painting, gardening, or cleaning. Above all, let that radiant stream of energy flow through your heart and lungs for revitalized breathing, circulation, and cleansing of the blood. This whole body experience of sexual energy has a powerful effect on our health, vitality, and our warm feelings about ourselves and others.

These suggestions can be easily misunderstood. I am suggesting neither a dematerialization nor a "spiritualization" of our sexuality. Nor am I suggesting that this whole body, diffused sexual experience is more holy than direct genital activity. Rather, I am suggesting that *none* of our powers and feelings need be wasted. When direct sexual activity is inappropriate, we can still accept the empowered gift in ways that bless us.

In the same disconcerting way, we often experience the energy of anger in a new way as our healing deepens. Anger in itself is not destructive unless it is the disguise for unfaced fear and inner woundedness. The anger that rises when we fully and honestly encounter the wounds within and around us can be a swift, clear, clean, energized thrust of the justice of love. It can become part of our confrontation with the bitterness of memory as that memory surfaces for healing. It can become part of the wisdom of our discernment. It can cleanse imbalanced relationships. It can be the empowered response of the "hunger and thirst for righteousness." It can become part of the dignity and compassion of our humanity.

The rising of this kind of anger, as with sexual awareness, is part of the growing, healing empowerment within our bodily selves. If it is unfaced, unreleased in creative ways, it can be deadly to our physical health and our relationships. If we never feel anger, we are probably out of touch with our feelings, and it may be that our healing has barely begun.

"Be angry but sin not," Paul wrote to the church in Ephesus (4:26), thus distinguishing between the anger

Healed Empowerment and Our Bodies

that is part of healing and the anger that is both a defense of fear and a weapon of attack.

We might ask ourselves the following questions concerning the nature of our anger:

Is anger my usual response in daily difficult situations?

Are the persons to whom I express my anger the ones who are really responsible for my feelings?

Have I learned to express my anger by saying "I feel . . ." rather than by "You are . . ."?

How do I feel about myself after expressing my anger?

Is there any creative change as a result of my expression of anger?

Do I avoid facing my inner unhealed wounds, thus not discovering what I'm really angry about?

Am I a person who sometimes gets angry—*or have I become an angry person*? If we suspect that much of our "righteous anger" is really a disguised desire to punish or a mask for our hurts and unexpressed needs, then we need (perhaps with the help of a counselor) to face our deep feelings in the presence of God's compassion and allow ourselves to be healed. As healed persons, anger will not leave our lives, but there will be a great change in the cause and nature of our anger as it becomes part of our health.

Even healthy anger, however, as with our sexuality, cannot always be overtly expressed. There are times when its open, direct expression might be inappropriate or damaging to another. At such times, we can learn to face what we feel, honor its presence, and locate where in our body lies the focus of the anger we feel. Is the anger felt most in our heart, our throat, our eyes, our jaw, our head, our abdomen, or our chest? When the anger's bodily center has been located, picture the offered vital power flowing like a clear radiant river of light through the whole body. Then, while slowly and deeply breathing, picture this energy flowing out through the palms of the hands and through the feet into the ground, asking God to help us use this energy wisely in our decisions and actions. Sooner or later, the energy of anger must be openly expressed in some way, but while we are being guided into the right timing, none of our energies need be wasted. They come as gifts.

Sometimes our growing wholeness of empowerment manifests itself as enthusiastic longing to eat, drink, play, dance, or exercise. Excess in any of these can be defensive escapes from self-encounter, but their exuberant expression also can rise from the released longing to taste more deeply the variety and delight of life. This is especially true when there have been deeply repressed and long unawakened powers.

Instead of denying newly awakened exuberance, we can explore ways by which this vitality can become a sacramental means of receiving God's life. We can focus lovingly on each bite of food, the movement of each muscle, each precious sight, sound, and fragrance. When quality begins to overtake quantity, we will become less concerned over the number of miles run, the amount of food served, the number of parties and meetings attended, the accumulation of our collectibles. We will become more lovingly aware of the quality of each one of the gifts of God.

Our gifted empowerment which rises and manifests in our bodies as we are healed comes for four main reasons:

that we may more thoroughly enter into the joy of God and may more fully taste the gifts of God;

76

that we may more fully encounter, accept, and embrace our unique identity;

that we may with passion and compassion bear one another's burdens and "wash one another's feet";

that we may be eager channels of the healing transformation that God longs to bring to the agony of the world.

Suggested Meditation for the Recognition and Blessing of Our Powers

They who wait for the Lord shall renew their strength, they shall mount up with wings like eagles.

—Isaiah 40:31

Arise, shine; for your light has come, and the glory of the Lord has risen upon you.

—Isaiah 60:1

Claim with thankfulness the promised presence of God's love through Christ. Spend some time in some of the suggested forms of nurturing prayer, visualizing and breathing God's light, or some other way of relaxing into the nearness and love of God.

Ask to become aware of any bodily manifestations of new growing powers and gifts such as suggested in this chapter. Thank your body for these signals and for helping channel to you these gifts.

Ask God for some symbolic form to indicate the presence and manner of our gifts. Now relax again and wait with expectancy. See if there comes some inner image, perhaps in the form of a child or a freshly growing shrub, in the symbol of a bird, a light, or a color. Perhaps some memory will surface which hints the nature of our gift or power, or perhaps some other thought or awareness will come. It does not matter if you do not immediately understand it. Visualize the Christ welcoming and interacting with the symbolic form of your empowerment. Allow the meditation to move as it will. Do not try too quickly to identify or name your gifts. Just rejoice in their presence. If nothing special seems to surface, just enjoy the nurturing prayer, express welcome to whatever gift God is bringing alive within you, and ask for some indication within the near future. (See what happens in the next few days that feels like guidance.)

Give thanks to God that, whether you become aware of your empowerment or not, it is there. As God deepens the healing, the powers must and will awaken. Thank your body and express trust in its signals. You may feel the need for tears or laughter during this prayer. You may become aware of sexual feelings. Anger may surface, as well as feelings of deep love and compassion. These are part of our empowered human praying and are blessed by God. When ready, conclude the meditation.

· 7 ·

Relating to Our Bodies in Illness and Disability

A book like this can sound complacent. It's all very well to write about the signals, powers, pleasures and participation of our bodies when all our bodily parts *are* able to move, respond, communicate, and cooperate. But what about our bodies when they are paralyzed, blind, deaf, lame? What about our bodies when they are in pain and weakness or trapped in progressive disease? Where is our communication and empowerment when our body feels quite literally a prison or even a torture chamber?

During this past decade, special thought and help has been given to the special problems of disability. (Rather than speaking of "disabled," we prefer to say *other-abled* or *physically challenged*.) Every day I see men and women going about their work in electrically-operated wheelchairs, guided by specially trained dogs, or learning to move and communicate through other ways and abilities. I have often talked with these men and women in our professional schools and have learned many things. To be other-abled is not necessarily the same thing as illness. One can be lame, paralyzed, blind, deaf, or mute and still be in basic good health. But the relationship of an other-abled individual with the body is of a unique poignancy.

For probably all of us, at least at times, being disabled hurts. Even if the larger community would adopt totally fair and appropriate attitudes toward people with disabilities, this would still not eliminate the sense of loss, the frustration, and indeed the anger we feel just because we are disabled. . . .

Because we are disabled, many of us have pretty low self-esteem. Our physical appearance, for example, often does not fit any traditional standards. . . . we cannot do one or more basic life function. This . . . can also be extremely demoralizing. . . .

. . . Positive thinking can, of course, be quite useful. . . . But if a newly-disabled woman is constantly surrounded by only those spouting worn-out "it could be worse" cliches, she is likely to develop a very strong urge to strangle them all. . . . nothing they can say or do can make that disability disappear. It's there, and it's real, and it must be coped with.[9]

So how does one relate to one's body? Is it really possible to *have* a vital, loving relationship with the bodily self at all under such circumstances?

"How do you manage? How do you feel about your body?" I recently asked a church leader who had permanently lost the use of both of her legs in a car accident. She was in an electrically-operated chair. A rather plump woman, she was dressed in warm attractive colors, and her eyes shone with enthusiasm for her work.

"My paralysis of my legs is a fact, a given," she answered bluntly. "It's a fact of my life now, just like the fact that I am short and have curly hair. Yes, I do sometimes think of the way I used to be, and yes, I do sometimes grieve bitterly. I had to face that and work through it. You can't cut short the grieving and the anger. You have to stay with it and work it through.

"But I don't need to *stop* there. I have gone on. My

body is my friend, more than ever. I can pray for it, relate to it. I communicate with it, and I feel a response. Maybe not in my legs any more, but they are still *my* legs, part of the family even if I can't feel them. There is still circulation going on there, cellular change. Yes, my legs, though paralyzed, are still working in many ways for the good of my whole body.

"I am relating to my body—just as much as you do, though I've had to learn new ways of relating. I thank my legs for the work they are still doing, and I ask the rest of my body to take over as much as possible their missing functions."

As I listened to her and to others with similar problems, I realized there *was* a real relationship with the body possible, a relationship in many ways much deeper than mine had ever been. I realized that though one bodily ability is cut off or limited, there are other powers, awarenesses, abilities that develop. This is why the word *other-abled* is a much more descriptive word than *disabled*.

A blind man once said to me some years after losing his sight, "I can hear more deeply what others are saying and feeling. It's as if I had a way of sensing or discerning that I didn't have before. I don't quite know where to locate this ability, or where in my body it's focused, but it is certainly real and very present."

We must neither misunderstand nor dishonor this kind of witness by thinking that there is no sense of loss, anger, or grieving. It is unrealistic and dangerous to try to gloss over our woundedness. I have recently read in the newspapers of a twenty-one-year-old girl who is totally paralyzed for life by a random bullet from a sniper. In one minute, a beautiful young body was rendered unmoving, bed-ridden for life. We have all heard of similar tragedies, and as we pray for them, we wonder how we would be feeling in their place: Longing for death? Grateful for life? Anger? Despairing loss? Grief beyond description? Acute awareness of the love of others? Determination? Anger at God? Closeness to God? Probably we would feel all of these at different times, or even simultaneously. These are fully human feelings, bodily, emotional, relational, honored and understood by God. This humanity of ours must be encountered and lived. One of the most powerful and comforting aspects of the Bible is that human feelings are never negated. Hatred, fear, loneliness, despair, and longing are fully expressed, with knowledge that God hears and understands. Just leaf through the Book of Psalms. No one is playing games with God or trying to repress or hide feelings in the Psalms! Jesus never hesitated to weep, feel anger, or express grief, need, or loneliness. To feel our feeling is a necessary part of our wholeness.

We must not make the mistake of thinking that God has sent us tragedy to punish us or to improve us. As a child, I used to listen to the singing of a powerful old song about a blind farmer. The whole song was in praise to God, who took away his sight so that his soul might see. Though I loved the beautiful melody, I worried a lot about that song. It made God seem scary and cruel. I hoped God wouldn't take any special notice of *me*! But as I grew older and began to read the New Testament, I noted that Jesus never refused to heal the blind because it was better for their souls. He never told anyone that God had sent illness upon them for their own good.

There were apparently times when Jesus *couldn't* heal very extensively or effectively, such as in his own home town of Nazareth: "He could do no mighty work there, except that he laid his hands upon a few sick people and healed them" (Mark 6:5). There are often blocks to our healing, but that is not God's wish for us. The God we see through Jesus is always on the side of healing and grieves for us and with us in our suffering.

Illness or other physical disasters are not the same as the cross that Christians are called to carry. These crosses are tasks of loving, sacrificial involvement with others, bearing their burdens. These are offered to us freely, and we are free to accept or reject them.

Our personal disasters are more like Paul's thorn in the flesh (2 Cor. 12:7-9) and may come for many different reasons in our lives, but never as God's will for us. There may be blocks to their removal, but God works with us for healing, even if they are, for some of us, life-long problems. We do not know why healing is sometimes so delayed, why it may come only in part, or why it perhaps may never come fully to our bodies. Recently a friend suggested to me that there might be a difference between being cured and being healed. I found this to be a helpful distinction. Perhaps the new creativity that God's grace helps us bring from our "thorns" is a healing, though the cure may not be complete in this life. Thus, in the midst of the "thorn" experience, we are promised freedom from bondage. Bondage is the feeling that our lives are out of control; that we have no choices or alternatives; that there is no more "new creation"; that we are living in captive obedience rather than in relationship. God sets us free to discover that each moment, within grace, opens endless creative possibilities.

We discover, as did my friend whose legs were paralyzed, that our bodies are a precious part of us. Our bodies are to be loved, not because of the problem (which would be masochistic), in spite of the problem (which would be patronizing), or even through the problem (which could be too idealistic). Rather our bodies should be loved within the problem, as part of our whole life's experience. Such a concept is expressed with unsurpassed poignant power in the book from which I quoted earlier in this chapter, *With the Power of Each Breath*:

> Our bodies are our most precious and often our only possessions. . . . Some of us live in chronic pain, some with chronic unpredictability, and others with chronic stares. . . We need to see our bodies as worthy parts of ourselves in order to invest the time and energy it takes to care for ourselves. . . . We are regarded as "defects."
> . . . Value judgments are assigned to our "good" and "bad" parts. . . . Our integrity as persons has been undermined. . . . We claim our bodies and our integrity as disabled women. We insist on our right to make informed decisions about our bodies. We do not have good parts, bad parts or inner beauty. We come in many sizes, shapes and colors. Our bodies deserve our love, tenderness and pleasure.[10]

Relating to the body while undergoing illness and pain often presents very different problems from those of disablement. (As indicated earlier, dis- or other-able ment may not necessarily involve pain or disease.) Illness and disease may be chronic or temporary, but there is always a sense of struggle and unease as the body works to cast off bacterial invasion or to regain its chemical balance and vitality. The very work the body is doing makes it hard for us to love and communicate with it. It is hard for us not to hate and repudiate our body when it signals extreme discomfort and pain. It is hard not to blame it, or at least to ignore and escape from it, by merely deadening the symptoms. When caught by the misery of even just a bad cold, I for one am all too apt to feel totally unspiritual, merely enduring with intense dislike the close presence of my struggling life partner, my body! I talked once with a woman who had several operations for recurring cancer, moving through them with unmatched courage and good cheer. But when she broke her little toe while vacationing on a beach, she reacted with complete outrage to the pain!

"I experienced more pain with that toe than I ever had in my cancer," she told me, both laughing and indignant. "My whole body hurt! I never realized how much weight we put on the foot and how much we take the foot for granted. I think I know now what Paul meant when he wrote that the head can't say to the feet 'I have no need of you.' But I still can't help being mad at my foot for hurting me so!"

How can we best relate to and communicate with our bodies at these times? Probably it is best not to try to engage in long, intense meditations, but it is essential to keep some form of repeated, encouraging thought going toward our bodies. Our bodies are working with full force to preserve and keep us well, like a brave friend carrying our burden and fighting our battles. It must be allowed to do its full work without distraction, but with awareness of our appreciative concern and with forms of encouragement and imagery that help along its brave struggle. This does not mean we do not face and express our feelings of anger and dismay. Open admission of feeling will not block the body in its work. Unadmitted feelings are far more unhealthy and damaging. But along with the admitted feeling, we can choose many ways of helping our bodies with our conscious focusing. Some suggest visualizing the immune system encountering and overcoming in various ways bacterial and viral invaders.

If our body is experiencing an organic imbalance or deficiency, it is helpful to speak lovingly and encouragingly to the main organic systems involved, thanking them for the work they do, envisioning the healing light or healing waters of God surrounding and permeating them. We do this in the same way we would pray for a friend carrying a hard burden or working through a problem. Ask your body what you, your conscious self, can do to help in the way of diet, rest, exercise, and daily life. Do not set timetables for healing, and do not push or force. We need to respect the body's own rhythm of timing and healing. Remind yourself that the body has not suddenly become your enemy. Your body has not attacked you. It, too, is undergoing attack. It is helping carry the burden of your spirit and the pain of your community.

Like a brave, wise friend who works closely with you, your body will give signals, suggestions, share its wisdom. Dr. Bernie Siegel, a surgeon specializing in cases of cancer, quotes the witness of a young pregnant woman recovering from a mastectomy, but knowing that cancer had spread to her lymph glands:

As soon as I left the hospital, I tried to listen to my insides. I wanted my body and mind to tell me how to help them survive. I got some answers, and I tried to follow them even when I was too depressed to move or care. My body said: "Drink orange juice," a curious craving I'd never experienced before. I drank and drank, and it felt right. . . . I told my food to make me strong. I told each vitamin . . . to go to the right places and do the right things. . . .

My body said, "Move, Lois, and do it fast!" Thirty minutes after I came home from the hospital I went for a walk.

I told my body through exercise that I loved it and wanted it to be healthy. . . .

My mind and body said, "Make love," and they were right. . . .

I told my body to be well. I told my immunological system to protect me. . . . I watched my blood flowing strongly. I told the wound to heal quickly and the area around it to be clean. . . .

I think of cancer every day, but I also think of how strong my body is, how good it feels most of the time. I still talk to my insides. I have a feeling of integration of body, mind and, probably, spirit, which I have never before experienced.[11]

Norman Cousins, in his book *The Healing Heart*, shares his own experience after his recovery from a massive heart attack:

The belief that illness is something that comes into us from the outside . . . is so firmly ingrained in us that we naturally look to available outside forces to do battle with it and evict it. Since we are attacked from without we tend to believe we can be rescued only from without. We have little knowledge of, and therefore little confidence in, the numberless ways the human body goes about righting itself. . . . What can the individual do? First of all, it is important to be aware of the body's natural drive to heal itself, once freed of the provocations that played a part in bringing on the illness. . . . Each individual presides over the totality of himself or herself.[12]

Above all, therefore, in times of illness, it is essential to be in close touch with the body's wisdom as it works for healing. And if we have entered into a warm, appreciative, listening relationship with our bodies before illness strikes, it is all that much easier to hear and cooperate.

In our close work with our bodily selves during illness, it is absolutely necessary not to fall into the trap of guilt, believing that we are personally, totally responsible for all of our illnesses. As I pointed out earlier, we *do* live in a world in which there are bacteria, viruses, pollution, and genetic problems, and we *do* live in human communities whose burdens and stresses we share. Up to a point, our unhealed stress and our unwise lifestyles can and do make us vulnerable to illness, but seldom does illness rise solely from our personal mistakes. In our excitement over the new options of claiming responsibility for our own bodies, sometimes we go too far and imply in our attitudes to others that they must have done something against the laws of God or nature, or they wouldn't be sick! This puts us right back into the errors of the "comforters" of Job. This is glib, simplistic, and ignorant of the mystery of interweaving between ourselves and our communities, ourselves and the problems of this universe in which we are embodied.

Somehow we must maintain the miracle of wholeness and healing when the body and mind work together in loving unity within God's embrace and at the same time acknowledge the presence of mystery, knowing that we do not have all the answers, knowing that God works ceaselessly with our body and mind to bring light out of darkness. This is a difficult balance, and yet it is the biblical challenge to us. There is excitement in God's unfolding work, in the realism that we have just begun and that there is so much to learn and, above all, that we are all bound together—God, humanity, the world around us, and worlds to come—in such love that if one suffers all suffer together, if one is healed, all share the life and joy.

With this humility always with us, let us move boldly into the exploration and excitement of the possibilities that unfold when we enter the new relationship of tenderness and fellowship with our bodies.

A minister shared recently that he called on a woman in the hospital who had had surgery and was recovering successfully in all areas but one; her bladder was not yet functioning. The doctors refused to release her from the hospital until it did. Each day she was getting angrier at her bladder for its behavior. The minister listened lovingly to her anger, and all of a sudden heard himself saying, "I can understand how you feel, but don't you think it's time now that you became *friends* with your bladder? Why don't you speak to it with love and encouragement and picture Jesus touching it with healing hands? Your bladder is your friend and needs your help." This was a totally new idea for the woman. That night she prayed this way for her body, and the next morning the bladder began to function spontaneously.

We do not always experience such a swift, complete response. The timing of our bodies is not always the same as that of our conscious mind. The body has to get in touch with the depths of our subconscious mind and do quite a lot of other work before the outer symptoms begin to change. But this change is set in motion when our attitude becomes friendly and encouraging. The body hears, and *something* always begins to happen, even if there is not always a complete cure.

Often one of the first changes we notice is in the pain level. When in pain, while sending loving messages to the bodily powers of healing, work also on the pain by visualizing the painful part of the body breathing in and out slowly, gently, as if it had its own mouth and nose. Try this with an arthritic finger. Either before or after doing your finger limbering exercises, let the finger lie relaxed and visualize your whole body breathing through that finger as if it had its own breathing organs and was inhaling the healing light of God through each breath. Let your finger breathe as long as feels comfortable and then return to your ordinary way of breathing.

Next, flex the finger. It is an almost incredible pain relief. This localized "breathing" is effective for any part of the body. (Naturally, continue to take any needed medication. God also reaches us through dedicated doctors, and many of God's miracles reach us through medical help.)

Never try to carry the burden of pain and illness alone. Not only does God's help reach us through medical means but also in profound ways through friends or a trusted prayer group. Ask others to hold you through their thoughts and prayers in God's healing light. The combined prayer of even a small group is of inexpressible power. It is significant how often Jesus, in his works of healing, called together a little group of faith, sometimes only two or three people, to help channel his healing power.

Thirty-five years ago, the Methodist minister and healer, Leslie Weatherhead, gave an example of how this can be effectively done:

My own method of offering intercession for the sick . . . is as follows: . . .

. . . I try to make an imaginative picture of what is actually happening. This is the kind of thing that was said in an actual case:

"Here is Nurse So-and-so, a member of our church, a girl of nineteen. . . . She is suffering from such-and-such a disease. Her temperature is very high. She cannot sleep without drugs. She has not taken any food for some days. In imagination . . . 'go into the ward and stand with Christ next to her bed. . . . Believe that at this very moment Christ is touching her life, and that His healing power is being made manifest in her body now. Believe that He can more powerfully work in the atmosphere of our faith and love.' " . . .

Sometimes I use the words: "Let your prayers do

what your arms would do if we lived in the days of Christ's presence on earth. We should carry the patient into His presence. Believe that your prayer is bringing the patient and Christ into living proximity and vital relationship."[13]

If healing is delayed or if it seems likely that it will not come fully in this life, never feel that you are disqualified from praying for others and helping to bring healing to others. This was again shown to me at a recent meeting I attended while in acute pain from lower back spasms. I sat next to a minister who, through neurological illness, had lost the use of his legs and was sitting in an electric wheelchair. He had a most observable loving radiance about him. In the midst of the meeting, my pain suddenly and dramatically left me.

"Did you pray for me?" I asked him afterwards.

"Yes," he answered quietly. "I observed that you were in discomfort, and I channeled God's healing light to you."

"Has this happened before?" I asked.

He hesitated, and then said, "Yes, I have noticed that sometimes God can use me to help others."

I think this was very much Paul's experience when the removal of his thorn in the flesh (whatever it was) was delayed, and he heard God saying to him, "My grace is sufficient for you" (2 Cor. 12:9). This does not mean that God wants anyone to be hurt or in wheelchairs, but rather that God can and does bring our lives into creative power even when healing is delayed.

This was an especially significant realization for Paul. The orthodox of many cultures and faiths in his time believed that physical imperfection disqualified a person from the full sacramental service of God and channeling from God. Unless you were a perfect physical specimen, you were considered neither to be in the true likeness of God nor worthy to be set apart sacrificially for sacramental service to God. Unfortunately, many today still believe or are told by others that if they are chronically ill or disabled, they cannot minister to others. It is not easy for the physically challenged to find churches willing to train and call them as pastors, though their experiences have enriched their powers of compassion and intuitive awareness.

Even in temporary illness, we often hesitate to work for the healing of others. It is true that, when ill, we must learn how to let ourselves receive and be nurtured, and we should not undertake strenuous forms of meditation or intercession. But a quiet visualization of others held in the healing light of God while we rest in bed, the quiet inner speaking of another's name along with the name of Jesus is prayer of great power.

Suggested Prayer for Our Bodies
When Permanently Other-abled or Chronically Ill

Now thus says the Lord, he who created you, . . . "Fear not, for I have redeemed you; I have called you by name, you are mine. When you pass through the waters I will be with you; and through the rivers, they shall not overwhelm you; when you walk through the fire you shall not be burned. . . ."

The Spirit of the Lord God is upon me, because the Lord has anointed me to bring good tidings to the afflicted; he has sent me to bind up the brokenhearted, to proclaim liberty to the captives, and the opening of the prison to those who are bound; . . . to comfort all who mourn; . . . to give them a garland instead of ashes, the oil of gladness instead of mourning, the mantle of praise instead of a faint spirit; that they may be called oaks of

righteousness. . . . they shall raise up the former devastations; they shall repair the ruined cities.
                                    —Isaiah 43:1-2; 61:1-4

Claim with thanksgiving the real and loving presence of Jesus Christ. Lean on that strength and breathe healing light as suggested in the other meditations. Encounter your true feelings with honesty and gentleness, knowing that God knows all about them and is so lovingly near. Visualize Jesus embracing your feelings of anger, grief, despair, loneliness, numbness. Now in the presence of Jesus, speak to the part of your body that is suffering or disabled: "Dear One, in many ways you are prevented from doing the full work that you long to do for the whole self. In many ways it is hard to feel your presence, and it is sometimes hard to love you. But you are still part of me. We still belong to each other. You are still in so many ways working for me. The blood still circulates within you, your cells breathe, and your skin protects me from bacteria. You are needed and valued. I bless you. Christ blesses you and touches you."

If such actual speaking to the affected parts of your body seems uncomfortable to you, just image that bodily part breathing in and out of the light of life for restoration of the quiet work it is still doing. Then let the whole body breathe.

If some bodily part, an arm, a leg, a breast, a prostate, a uterus, has had to be removed due to accident or surgery, do not just think of it as rotting trash carried away and thrown out. This bodily part served you, and for the good of the whole it had to be removed, sacrificed. I believe we should think lovingly and gratefully of that sacrificed member, remembering the times of its strength and presence, being glad we had it. Speak to the body as a whole, and encourage it to take with joy and willingness as much of the function and activity of the removed member as possible. It is almost incredible how the body cells and organs respond to that kind of loving challenge in their compensating work.

Suggested Meditations for Any Illness and/or Pain

Preserve me, O God, for in thee I take refuge. . . . I have no good apart from thee. . . . I bless the Lord who gives me counsel; in the night also my heart instructs me. I keep the Lord always before me; . . . I shall not be moved. Therefore my heart is glad, and my soul rejoices; my body also dwells secure. . . . Thou dost show me the path of life; in thy presence there is fulness of joy, in thy right hand are pleasures for evermore.
—Psalm 16:1-2, 7-9, 11

The Lord is my shepherd, I shall not want. . . . He restores my soul.
—Psalm 23:1, 3

"Beloved Christ who understood and entered into the flesh and all its problems, breathe on me your healing breath and touch me with your healing hands. In your presence I speak to my body: 'Dear one, I can't feel very happy with you right now. I am hurting, and I feel weak. It is hard to use the strength even to speak to you. I know I feel this way because you are fighting a hard battle for me. You have called up all of your deep vital powers to make me well again. I thank you, I honor and trust you, both in your work that I understand and in the work that goes far beyond what I see and feel.

" 'I will try to relax, to trust, to cooperate with all you are doing. Send me signals of what I can do to help you. Now put around us Christ's healing cloak of light, covering the whole self in warmth and peace. I see any painful areas breathing this peace gently in and out.'"

Or: Just lie quietly, letting the painful areas breathe in and out slowly and quietly while thinking of the words of Jesus: "My sheep hear my voice, and I know them, . . . and no one shall snatch them out of my hand" (John 10:27), or the words of the beautiful old hymn: "Breathe on me, Breath of God. Fill me with life anew." Visualize God holding you and doing the breathing for you while you rest. This form of meditative, restorative prayer can either go on for hours or just for a few minutes several times a day.

Or: Relax your body, breathing gently for a few minutes. Picture a light shining deep within your body, perhaps at the heart center, in the very center of the brain, or in some other center of the body that seems right to you. The light may be white, gold, rose, or some other color. Watch the light within your body for a while, and then visualize it beginning to flow like a powerful river of light to bodily parts that are in pain or stress. Now see it expanding more and more fully and flowing throughout the whole body, bringing healing with its flowing power.

This is the healing power springing deeply from within *you*, the power God has put in our marvelous bodies. While so visualizing, you might wish to repeat this prayer:

> For with thee is the fountain of life; in thy light do we see light.
>
> —Psalm 36:9

You can use the imagery of water instead of light, or any other imagery God gives you in your heart.

8

The Healing and Renewal of Our Community Body

The church members were gathered for a closing communion service in the little log cabin chapel among the redwood trees near the California coast. We had shared three days of conversation, prayer, singing, laughter, games, and hiking during this family retreat. At this last prayer service, a young father and mother brought forward their five-month-old daughter, wasted by some undiagnosed illness. I had noticed that the baby had been brought to all the meetings, always held in her father's or mother's arms. I had noticed her pale little face and gentle smile but had not been told of her illness until the second day. The day after the retreat she was to be taken to the hospital for extensive tests.

The pastor suggested that the whole church family gather around closely. While he laid gentle hands on the baby, praying, the church members touched him, the parents, or each other. An unbroken channel of healing love surrounded the baby and her parents.

It was quiet in the chapel, though many of the members were weeping. The presence of the living Christ was very near, and we all felt the closeness of the healing light. God's arms were around us all.

As we quietly prayed, I thought of Jesus going into the room where the little daughter of Jairus lay. I remembered how Jesus brought into the room with him the child's father, mother, and three of his disciples, thus forming a little community of faith so that the radiant nearness of God's healing love might be experienced with more intensity (Luke 8:49-55).

Never before had I felt so poignantly the significance and the power of the presence of the church, Christ's body on earth. The health of a community body depends so utterly on its tenderness and its honor towards all its members. As Paul wrote to Corinth, comparing the community body to the physical body (just a few verses before breaking into his great hymn of love in the thirteenth chapter), "God has so composed the body . . . that there may be no discord in the body, but that the members may have the same care for one another. If one member suffers, all suffer together; if one member is honored, all rejoice together" (1 Cor. 12:24-26).

It is in community that our true faith is revealed and tested. Just as our spirituality must be experienced in our personal bodies, so must it also be experienced in our community bodies. If our spirituality has become merely an individualistic exercise—if our whole self (body, emotions, spirit) is not part of our community context—we have missed the meaning of the incarnational life. In the chapter on our empowerment, I quoted God's promise in Isaiah 58: "Then shall your light break forth like the dawn." This promise follows the challenge that followers of God are

> to let the oppressed go free,
> and to break every yoke. . . .
>   to share your bread with the hungry,
> and bring the homeless poor into your house;
> when you see the naked, to cover him,
> and not to hide yourself from your own flesh.
>   —Isaiah 58:6-7

This prophetic utterance speaks of community health, the community within our own bodies and feelings, and the community of others around us. We have not genuinely experienced one if we have not experienced the other.

The nurture, inclusiveness, and sensitivity which we try to bring to our own bodies is precisely the same nurture, inclusiveness, and sensitivity we are asked to bring to our community body. All members are to be heard. All members are to be honored, nurtured, valued, encouraged, prayed for and with. The members we have thought to be weak may actually be the strongest. The members who have served in silent faithfulness are to be noted and thanked. The members who are in pain need special nurture. The members that seem disabled are *other*-abled and work quietly for the whole body. Those of which we have been ashamed need to be seen and recognized as part of our whole selves. It is impossible to separate the way we feel about ourselves from the way we feel about one another.

Our refusal to hear, our indifference, and our rejections tell much more about *us* than they do about those whom we reject. I often think with sadness about a man in our community who died a few years ago. For years he had been a neighborhood problem. He drifted from group to group (every prayer group in town knew him well!), always hopeful that this time he would find an ultimate answer, this time the miracle of abundant life would come to him. Always he related to others by "latching on," trying to find someone who would take emotional responsibility for him and tell him what to do.

Because of the very urgency of his need, the man was emotionally and physically unattractive. Most of us went far out of our way to avoid him because we didn't know how to relate to him. We found him extremely draining and parasitical. When we *had* to encounter him, we would listen with superficial kindness and escape as soon as possible. We did not take him seriously as a human being or relate to him honestly from our own humanity. We were kindly, patronizing, detached. No one ever said an unkind word, but he was a most throughly rejected member of the community body.

I am glad that in the years just before his early death, he finally did find a church family in which he was given tasks to do that were valued and in which some of the members took him seriously enough to share their feelings. They explained gently to him how he affected others and suggested to him better ways to relate to others.

How often is our politeness merely a way of distancing ourselves from honest encounter? If we learn honesty within our own bodies and hearts, can we at last begin to learn it with one another?

The agony of the homeless is found in many of our communities. Often when we are coming from our big inner-city churches, we shudder to see men and women rolled up in ragged coats and sleeping in the grass, in doorways, under overpasses. How often we try to console ourselves, thinking that these must be alcoholics, drug addicts, or "substance abusers." There is nothing we can really do to help them, we decide. They would just end up in the same way.

Slowly, however, it begins to dawn on us that many of these homeless are not addicts or alcoholics at all, but men and women caught by the trap of unemployment and its vicious assaults on human hope and dignity. It is inexcusable that big cities that can afford orchestras and ballparks cannot, at the very least, afford warm shelters at night for the homeless.

How long it takes us to learn the simplest of facts: whether in our bodies or in our communities, if any one single member is unheard, unvalued, unnurtured, abandoned, abused, the whole body is sick!

Within the healthy community there is not only nurture for its members, but also openness towards new members, new ideas, new ways of living. A healthy family is not a closed circle; it reaches beyond itself in interest and concern or its spirit will die.

Often Jesus must have heard in the synagogue the passionate inclusiveness of the words of the prophet Isaiah concerning the "foreigner." A "foreigner" is any new, unencountered, *different* person, idea, or way of life which God challengingly presents to us, testing our love and our freedom.

> Let not the foreigner who has joined himself to the Lord say, "The Lord will surely separate me from his people." . . . The foreigners who join themselves to the Lord, to minister to him, to love the name of the Lord, . . . these I will bring to my holy mountain, and make them joyful in my house of prayer; . . . for my house shall be called a house of prayer for all peoples. Thus says the Lord God, who gathers the outcasts of Israel, I will gather yet others to him besides those already gathered.
>
> —Isaiah 56:3, 6-8

We hear this passionate inclusiveness again when Peter was called by vision to go to the Roman centurion Cornelius, enter his home, and claim him as brother in Christ, saying, "God has shown me that I should not call any man common or unclean" (Acts 10:28). We can hardly imagine how almost unheard of and radical this was for an orthodox Jewish man! We see the power of inclusiveness again in explicit fullness when Paul cried out to the church of Ephesus:

100

Now in Christ Jesus you who once were far off have been brought near in the blood of Christ. For he is our peace, who has made us both one, and has broken down the dividing wall of hostility. . . . So then you are no longer strangers and sojourners, but you are fellow citizens with the saints and members of the household of God.
—Ephesians 2:13-14, 19

Are we allowing God's Spirit to open our hearts and eyes to the "foreigner"? In what ways are our bodies, our personal lives, our families, our attitudes, and our communities still fragmented by the "dividing walls of hostility"?

This does not mean that we are all to act alike, think alike, or look alike, any more than the feet try to look like hands, or the nose like an ear. We each are unique in appearance and task and gift. It does, however, mean that all are equally heard, valued, and nurtured.

It is one thing to challenge us into inclusive loving. It is quite another to help us *do* it! This is agonizingly true when unhealed wounds and angers have been passed down for decades or centuries, when the roots of our hurt and anger reach far deeper than our personal lives. At a retreat one of the pastors stood and said in anguish: "I am a Christian, and I believe with all my heart in love and forgiveness. I want all other human beings to be my brothers and sisters. But I am an Armenian. How can I forgive the cold-blooded slaughter of thousands of Armenian civilians and love those who did it even though it was many years ago? It is all very well to claim oneness in Christ, but how can it become a reality for me with these inner wounds still bleeding?"

There were no easy answers. In fact, I don't think anyone tried to answer him. We shared his pain in love. Later some of us remembered what Henri Nouwen wrote in his powerful little book *The Wounded Healer*:

> A Christian community is therefore a healing communi-
> ty not because wounds are cured and pains are allevi-
> ated, but because wounds and pains become openings
> or occasions for a new vision. Mutual confession then
> becomes a mutual deepening of hope, and sharing
> weakness becomes a reminder to one and all of the com-
> ing strength.[14]

Indeed, on this occasion a new vision did begin to
dawn within me. I realized that prayer for our personal
inner wounds was only the beginning. I began to see
that until we started to encounter *communal* wounds of
unhealed memory, peace is not possible on this earth
any more than it is within our bodily and emotional
selves. Are not our wars, our riots, our plots, suspi-
cions, arms races, all signals and symptoms that our
community bodies are still suffering and bleeding from
unhealed agony, unhealed hostility, and mutual as-
saulting over many centuries? Just as our physical
bodies send us signs through pain, fever, and malfunc-
tion, so do our communal bodies.

What if we began to *listen*? What if we began to pray,
not just for the surface symptoms, but for the depths of
pain and dis-ease? What if, at long last, we finally faced
the heart-rending fact that "they have healed the
wound of my people lightly, saying, 'Peace, peace,'
when there is no peace" (Jer. 6:14).

Can we learn so to live and pray that we no longer try
to heal wounds lightly, superficially, but together reach
for the very roots of the pain? Would forgiveness begin
to be possible? Would peace become a reality? Is this
what God has been telling us through the Incarnation
and Christ's passion to heal?

Let us in our churches, prayer groups, and personal
prayers begin with boldness to explore in depth these

new frontiers of prayer for the radical healing of our family bodies, our church bodies, our racial, national, professional bodies. There is no limit to the possibilities. Any depth prayer is powerful; *communal* depth prayer is power inconceivable. We have everything to hope for if we move beyond our tight, timid walls of accustomed prayer and let God lead us into the excitement and transformation of what prayer was meant to be. This is one of the greatest empowered gifts offered to us.

Think what might happen if wounded, hostile family members began to pray for the healing of memories, the healing of traumas in the family tree, visualizing the loving Christ walking back through time to encounter, touch, heal the hurts of long ago.

Think of the possibilities if our church denominations began to pray for the indescribable hurts of religious wars and persecutions.

What if members of different races and nations began to pray for the centuries of mutually-inflicted pain? Not only would profound channels be opened to God's longing to heal, but as the healing of the deep pain expanded, forgiveness would, perhaps for the first time, become possible, and we would be released to the possibility of outer reconciling acts.

As with any form of intercessory prayer, there are some essential foundations. First, God is the healer. "Abide in me, and I in you," Jesus said. "As the branch cannot bear fruit by itself, unless it abides in the vine, neither can you, unless you abide in me. I am the vine, you are the branches" (John 15: 4-5). We are to be the transmitters, not the generators, of the healing light and energy. Constantly, as pastor and then as prayer group leader, I would forget this and try to be the source of limitless good will, vitality, power, and the answer to everyone's problems. No wonder after a few years of this I began to dread the evenings of the prayer groups and would end the evening chilly, irritable, and dying for a sugar fix! It was hard to allow myself to be just a human being in need of healing and nurture, a sheep as well as a shepherd.

Secondly, it is essential that we face our true feelings about the person or the group or the situation. If we feel dislike, reluctance, fear, resentment, we must admit those feelings to a loving God. If we are praying in a group about someone's illness, it is well if someone in the group reminds us that we are all apt to be nervous about getting sick ourselves. The feeling itself will never be a block to God's work of healing if it is faced. Unexpressed feelings can and do get in the way and are sometimes picked up by the very person for whom we are praying!

It is not necessary to force ourselves to feel love or liking for the one for whom we are praying. Just as suggested earlier, if there are parts of our bodies we dislike, we can't push ourselves into appropriate feelings. Rather we admit what we feel to God (who does not condemn our humanness) and let God do the loving. Usually when we release ourselves in this way, our feelings of dislike will themselves be healed.

Finally, as indicated in chapter 4, our prayer is not meant to be either diagnostic or prescriptive. We usually cannot tell what the foundational problem in any situation is, and though we may know of many hurts, we do not know of them all or which are the most significant. Neither can we know in what ways or timing healing will begin to come. There will be changes, but they are not always what we expected, and they do not always come at the time we expect. It is enough to know that there *is* a change, beginning at depth, when we have released a problem or person into the hands of the healing Christ and surrounded it with healing light by our channeling and focusing. The divine "yeast," the healing power is radically at work at the very center of the person and the problem.

Suggested Meditation for Inclusiveness in Our Communal Body

Beloved, let us love one another; for love is of God. . . . He who does not love does not know God; for God is love.

—1 John 4:7-8

Speaking the truth in love, we are to grow up in every way into . . . Christ, from whom the whole body, joined and knit together by every joint . . . , when each part is working properly, makes bodily growth and upbuilds itself in love.

—Ephesians 4:15-16

Relax your body and give thanks for the presence of Jesus Christ. Spend some nurturing moments breathing quietly the breath of life, surrounding your body with light. Think of some group to which you belong: family, church, professional, recreational. Think of some member of that group who has been ignored or unnurtured; or think of some "outsider" who has been neglected, unwelcomed, or even rejected. Share with Christ your honest feelings about this person and this situation.

Now visualize the Christ coming forth from your group and encountering this person or persons with welcome, embracing, listening, comforting, healing. Watch the encounter. Now the Christ turns to you and invites you to interact with this person. Do not force yourself in any way, but see what natural, spontaneous acts do occur and see if any warmth begins to grow.

Now visualize the other group members beginning to respond to this person in various ways. What is the person doing? How is the Christ interacting with all of you? This may be a prayer to which you need to return many times. Do not force any special scenario or conclusion. See what begins to happen spontaneously and what begins to grow. Ask to be shown in what ways you can personally help by your actions in the future.

Relax your body again and breathe quietly, leaning on the loving nearness of God through Christ. Share with Christ any special feelings of discomfort and difficulty you felt in this meditation. When ready, conclude the prayer.

Suggested Meditation for Deep, Unhealed Communal Memory

Thus says God, the Lord . . . I have taken you by the hand and kept you . . . to open the eyes that are blind, to bring out the prisoners from the dungeon, from the prison those who sit in darkness. . . . Behold, the former things have come to pass, and new things I now declare; before they spring forth I tell you of them.
—Isaiah 42:5-7, 9

Awake, O sleeper, and arise from the dead, and Christ shall give you light.
—Ephesians 5:14

Enter for a few moments into some form of relaxing, nurturing prayer. Let the love of Jesus Christ come to you in whatever symbolic form that is nearest and most powerful to you. Put around you the full light of healing and protection. Ask to have brought to your mind some group or community of which you are a part that you feel is suffering from unhealed wounds of the past (whether distant or recent past).

Walk with Christ to some symbolic entrance to these buried memories, and give consent that Christ goes through that entrance with full healing power. Do not try to go in also unless you feel especially summoned. Stand outside the entrance, giving thanks that the healing work of Christ (the love has *always* been there) is powerfully at work, encountering and touching the pain which is so deep that it is only partly known consciously.

When it seems the right time, visualize the Christ coming forth from the entrance, but leaving behind some strong symbolic form of the healing fire deep within the group memory.

Take several minutes to relax and breathe in the healing, restoring light around you, and when ready, conclude the prayer.

This second meditation is probably best done with a group. Far more healing power is released in the consent and channeling of a group (no matter how small), and since the communal pain which is being encountered at depth by the Christ is far vaster than our individual pain, it is best to have the reinforcement of a loving group around you.

9

Prayer for the Body of the Earth

Our retreat group stood in the redwood grove, breathing the evergreen scent and watching the sunlight shaft through the arches of the giant trees. We felt so blessed and nurtured by these trees that had surrounded our little group for our three days together. The pastor said to me, "We barely saved this grove, you know. Just a few years ago, it was slated for the axe. A group of us had to fight for it, and it was a near thing!"

I had not heard about that. I looked around at these towering, living, friendly presences and thought of what I had once read that someone had said about a grove of doomed trees, "They pay no taxes. They have no voice but the wind."[15]

As I write this, I have before me three recent newspaper clippings which are frightening. One article claims that many forms of life on earth are being ravaged by mass extinction, which annually destroys 17,500 species of plants and animals! It points out how endangered are the tropical forests, and how, if they are totally destroyed, our environment of air and earth will be radically changed.

Another article tells of the chemical and environmental imbalance caused by the increase of acid rain that strips away the waxy, protective coating of leaves, thereby upsetting the metabolic balance and signals of the trees. Thousands of maple, apple, birch, and spruce trees are sick and dying.

A third article points out the increasing evidence that the ozone layer around the earth's atmosphere, which provides the necessary protective filter from the rays of the sun, is deeply endangered, probably by the industrial use of chlorofluorocarbons, which also endangers the health of all living beings on this earth.

The body of our mother-father, earth itself, is giving grave warnings and signals of severe imbalance and impending illness. Our earth body, with its atmosphere, its water, its soil, its shrubs, trees, grass, animal life, is as much a bodily self as we are. What kind of relationship have we maintained with this precious body that has nurtured and sustained the human race for thousands of years?

At best, we have taken it for granted, used it, manipulated it. At worst, we have assaulted it, ravaged it, and, for immediate gain, destroyed many forms of its life with careless unconcern, poisoning its air, water, and soil. It seems almost incredible that eight hundred years ago a prophetic German cloistered sister, a spiritual leader of her time, Hildegard of Bingen, wrote two such appropriate meditations:

> Now in the people
> that were meant to green,
> there is no more life of any kind.
> There is only shrivelled barrenness.
>
> The winds are burdened
> by the awful stink of evil,
> selfish goings-on.
>
> . . . .

The air belches out
the filthy uncleanliness of the peoples.

There pours forth an unnatural,
a loathsome darkness,
that withers the green,
and wizens the fruit
that was to serve as food for the people.

Sometimes this layer of air
is full,
full of fog that is the source
of many destructive and barren creatures,
that destroy and damage the earth,
rendering it incapable
of sustaining humanity.

The earth should not be injured.
The earth should not be destroyed.[16]

Only in recent decades has there been evidence of rising communal awareness and alarm. Will we be in time? This is not only an ecological issue, a survival issue, but also a spiritual issue! As we relate anew to our bodily selves, we begin to feel an urgency to relate anew to the body of our earth. As with our bodies, our earth was never meant to be a prison of the soul. It is an ancient, curiously persistent heresy that demonic forces were responsible for creating this world and that God saves us by detaching us from earth, this dungeon for unreleased spirits. Though this was condemned as a heresy centuries ago, it still influences us. Many spiritual groups today show the effects of this ancient teaching. Some modify the outright repudiation of this earth into an attitude of indifference and detachment. If the earth is not an actual prison of the soul, they argue, at least it is not relevant to the soul, and the less we are concerned with it, the holier we become!

Others modify this feeling further, admitting that, after all, the earth might be considered a gymnasium of the soul, a testing house, a mechanical means by which moral muscle might be developed. In this way, earth might be helpful, but it has not value or life in itself. When our souls are finished with it, we can kick it away indifferently like an outworn piece of equipment!

These attitudes are astonishingly and significantly similar to the various mechanistic and depersonalized attitudes many of us have toward our bodies. Hard as it is for us to rethink and refeel our bodies as faithful companions, part of our wholeness, part of our spiritual growing, it may be even harder for us to relate to our earth's body as the essential, nurturing, ancient companion of our spiritual, somatic journey. Our earth is not God, any more than our bodies are God, and earth itself, even as our bodies, needs our healing and prayer as much as we need its healing and prayer. Any assault, manipulation, depersonalization of our earth is even more destructive to our humanity than is the depersonalization of our own bodies.

But there is hope. There is still abundant life and signals of life in our mother-father earth, as well as signs of distress and sickness. Underlying both the active, outer witness of our urgent concern for animals, plants, soil, and air and the public, legal, and political influences we must build to save us all, there must grow the foundational attitudes and loving, humanized faith.

Turning again to Hildegard of Bingen as she speaks to us from the twelfth century:

Prayer and Our Bodies

And as human persons view creation
                with compassion,
                in trust,
they see the Lord.

. . . .

Does not humanity know that God
is the world's creator?

With nature's help,
humankind can set into creation
all that is necessary and life sustaining.

. . . .

This is possible,
possible through the right and holy
                utilization of the earth,
the earth in which humankind has its
                source.

The sum total of heaven and earth,
everything in nature,
is thus won to use and purpose.
It becomes a temple and altar
for the service of God.[17]

In other words, nothing short of compassion and trust as we encounter the earth's body will heal the deep alienation from our living soma-source. We must be open to a new communal bond with all the living forms of life around us.

How can our life of prayer heal and help us in this urgent need for relationship with the earth? I believe a first step is to realize that just as our bodies hear and respond to our thoughts, feelings, and intentionality, so does the earth. Just as we can send love and encouragement to every cell, every organ, every bodily member, so can we send such love to the animals, trees, grass, and shrubs. That pioneer of spiritual healing, Agnes Sanford, had no hesitation whatever in using different manifestations of praying for the earth-body itself and all that is in it, from speaking to the weather and laying on of hands for earthquake faults, to communicating lovingly with her garden.

> But roses do not have ears that they may hear! No, of course they don't. However they do have within them that same light or energy of God that He breathed into man at the creation (Gen. 2:7). Therefore even without ears they can catch the feeling of words, the energy released through words, and can respond to it. . . .
> We have heard of people . . . for whom all plants seem to grow. The power within them is not a "green thumb," but it is that light of God flowing forth on the thought waves of love to the plants which they tend, and to the earth itself, the creation on which we live.

The earth not only hears us, we also hear the earth. This parallels the way in which our bodies not only hear our thoughts and feelings, but we begin to learn to listen to our bodies. A friend of mine goes for a walk when she is tired or depressed or puzzled by something and holds her open palms near blooming shrubs, newly opened leaves, or new-grown pine needles to feel the loving energy flowing into her body from the plants.
Matthew Fox tells us:

> To make contact with wisdom is to go beyond human words. . . .
> According to Von Rad, . . . "creation not only exists, it also discharges truth." Imagine that—creation itself, and not just books, is a source of truth and revelation. . . .

One is reminded, when hearing of how nature loves us, of a stanza from Baudelaire:

> We walk through forests of physical things
> that are also spiritual things
> that look on us with affectionate looks.

Notice how abundant the creative energy of God is—we do not walk just through *a* forest but all our lives long through *forests* of physical things that love us and pour out truth to us. But are we listening? Are we awake?[19]

In his stupendous and lyrical *Hymn of the Universe*, the Jesuit scientist Pierre Teilhard de Chardin meditates on the God-willed marriage between created matter and our human spirits:

> Steep yourself in the sea of matter, bathe in its fiery waters, for it is the source of your life. . . .
> . . . You hoped that the more thoroughly you rejected the tangible, the closer you would be to the spirit . . . ? Well, you were like to have perished of hunger. . . .
> . . . To understand the world knowledge is not enough, you must see it, touch it, live in its presence and drink the vital heat of existence in the very heart of reality. . . .
> . . . Till the very end of time matter will always remain young, exuberant, sparkling, new-born for those who are willing. . . .
> Oh, the beauty of spirit as it rises up adorned with all the riches of the earth!
> . . . Bathe yourself in the ocean of matter. . . . For it cradled you long ago in your preconscious existence; and it is that ocean that will raise you up to God.[20]

Just as warm fellowship with our physical bodies does not ignore the need for food, shelter, cleanliness

and medical care, these summons to deepen our root-
edness and fellowship with our earth-body are in no
way a quiescent turning from the hard work of saving
and sustaining our earth. Loving relatedness gives
meaning to our active work. A healthy marriage does
not consist only of adequate bed, board, and legal
fidelity. These are only the bare bones. Without love to
animate the union, without the passion of justice by
which the powers of each spouse are heard and valued,
the work of maintaining a household comes down to
mere survival tactics. Underlying our survival is the
danger and the glory of the balance and union of polarities within love.

Suggested Meditation for Bonding with and Listening to the Earth-Body

Praise the Lord from the earth.
—Psalm 148:7

The earth is the Lord's and the fulness thereof.
—Psalm 24:1

Let the earth rejoice; let the sea roar, and all that fills it;
let the field exult, and everything in it! Then shall all the
trees of the wood sing for joy before the Lord.
—Psalm 96:11-13

Lie on the ground, with your body fully held and
cradled by the earth. Rest, breath quietly, and picture
(and perhaps feel) the warm, loving currents of life and
healing streaming up from the earth's vitality into your
body. Let these currents of life stream into all parts of
your body, especially any areas that are tired or under

stress. This is God's gift through the fullness of the earth. Do you feel a relief of pain and stress?

Now place your palms on the ground, thank the ground, and bless it inwardly for all it gives. In this act of love, it is not only you laying on hands; the earth is doing the same for you! Are any new thoughts or insights rising within you?

Walk slowly and thoughtfully, holding your palms to the energy field of the growing shrubs, touching the strength of the trees, and letting the rich colors of flowers and grass nurture you. Let the colors flow into and through your body like healing streams and ask the flowing light to go in your body where it is most needed. When you return from your walk, relax and ask yourself if anything new has come to you.

Visualize the earth, which has given to you, held in God's arms.

Suggested Meditation for the Healing of the Body of the Earth

In God's hand are the depths of the earth; the heights of the mountain are his also.

—Psalm 95:4

O thou who hearest prayer! To thee shall all flesh come. . . . O God of our salvation, who art the hope of all the ends of the earth.

—Psalm 65:2, 5

Picture the love and light of God through Christ enfolding you in whatever way is best for you. Breathe quietly, and rest on God's strength. Now visualize the globe of the earth held in the loving hands of God and healing light flowing from God's hands into the earth's body, permeating every part. Picture the earth-body trustfully breathing in the light, just as your own body does. Hold this inner picture, giving thanks.

Now think of some special area of our earth which is badly wounded by war, industrial pollution, earth-quake, storm, fire, or disease. Picture (or inwardly witness to) the presence of Jesus Christ there, with full power, loving, blessing, and healing.

Ask to be shown some way in which you can also outwardly help in this problem. Visualize again the light around your own body, healing and sustaining. Breathe quietly, and when ready, conclude the prayer.

As with prayer for our community bodies, this prayer is especially powerful when prayed by a dedicated group. Some groups put a globe of the earth in the center of the circle to help maintain the focus. I believe that prayer groups everywhere should always include some form of prayer for the earth itself.

• 10 •

Daily Life in Prayer
with Our Bodies

When we enter into new relationship with our bodies, it doesn't matter if we are eight or eighty. Our bodies will know and gratefully respond. Many older people feel that it is too late to begin again with their bodily selves. They are having problems with hearing and sight, painful joints, or great fatigue. Some feel that old age is, by definition, a time of illness and weakness and that the body is past its best and on the downhill road.

Other older people are rediscovering themselves and their bodies in a new and joyful way, now that the heavy responsibilities of business and child-rearing are over.

"I had thought that my body would just close up shop," one woman in her late sixties told me. "But it's not that way at all. I love to walk, dance, swim, and feel my body moving and stretching slowly and rhythmically. Sometimes I put on a record and dance when I'm alone. I feel more sexual awareness than I did in my forties! There are some things through the day that I don't do as well or as quickly, but there are other things I do *better!*"

A man in his eighties told me, "I've learned not to demand or pressure myself. I don't force my eyes to read as long or my stomach to take in as much food. I don't insist that my muscles do hours of heavy work. I'm gentler with myself. I have bodily pleasures that are new to me. I notice these when I touch things: warm sunlight, flowers, rough tree bark, animal fur, soil on my hands when I work in the garden, and the grass under my bare feet. I like to listen to the wind blowing and the rain drops. It's like a whole new world!"

Was old age meant by God to be the flowering time of our sensory experience? It's an exciting thought! Even if we are not in good health in later years, it is never too late to begin a warm, appreciative friendship with our bodies, praising them for what they *are* able to do, listening to their suggestions and signals, thanking them for a lifetime of service, remaining open to new possibilities of delight and growing. We may be very sure that our bodily cells and organs hear our loving thoughts and will respond in many surprising ways.

Of course, the earlier we start this friendship, the easier and more natural it will seem. Even babies and little children can be helped to feel pride and love for their bodies and taught how to hear their body signals. Even in the heavy work of our middle years, there are ways by which we can build into our daily lives this appreciative awareness of our bodily selves.

I was talking with a friend, Cindy Winton-Henry, a teacher of theology and art and a pastor of the Christian Church (Disciples of Christ), who told me that while recently driving on the freeway, hastening from one meeting to another, she suddenly felt overwhelming gratitude for the privilege of being embodied, to be identifiable, to experience limits as a unique creation. "We enter into the spiritual through this gift of embodiment," she said thoughtfully. "I can't imagine having any spiritual experience which isn't also a bodily experience."

If we can remember our embodiment with awe and gratitude while driving on the freeway, cooking, washing, cleaning house, making love, preaching a sermon, reading a book, or talking with a friend, then we have entered into a unity with our bodies that has become a genuine marriage.

What are some ways by which we can daily deepen this relationship? The only methods and disciplines that really help us are the ones that grow out of our own unique way of relating. If the following suggestions are not right for your type and timing, ask God to unfold to you ways that are spontaneous and natural for you. These suggestions are alternatives meant to stimulate your *own* thinking and experimenting.

Waking and Rising

When I awake, I am still with thee.
—Psalm 139:18

Allow your body and your consciousness to respond gently to the new day. Try not to assault yourself with loud alarms and frantic leapings from bed. Gently stretch, lightly massage your face, neck, hands, and arms. Visualize God's renewing light flowing through your body. Lay your hands on your heart and picture the light expanding within. Tune in to your body's signals. Is there stiffness or discomfort anywhere? If so, touch that bodily part lovingly and let it breathe of the light. Picture your body moving with joy and strength out of the bed and, when ready, move into your projected image.

Cleansing

How precious is thy steadfast love, O God! . . . They feast on the abundance of thy house, and thou givest them drink from the river of thy delights. For with thee is the fountain of life.

—Psalm 36:7-9

Thou visitest the earth and waterest it, thou greatly enrichest it.

—Psalm 65:9

As you drink the morning's first water, as your body cleanses itself inwardly through elimination, and as you wash your outer body, become appreciatively aware of this refreshing, pleasurable cleansing. These are healthy, holy experiences and are meant (as with any act of holiness) to be enjoyed. Water on the body is an ancient, sacramental symbol of God's love and healing flowing out to human beings and to all living things. Many people find that they pray best and most fully and can feel God's response most clearly when in the shower!

Eating and Drinking

As they were eating, [Jesus] took bread, and blessed, and broke it, and gave it to them. . . . And he took a cup, and when he had given thanks he gave it to them, and they all drank of it.

—Mark 14:22-23

These are the beloved, well-known words of our communion service and our sacrament of the Lord's Supper. In the earliest days of the church, this service was incorporated into a real supper, an *agape* feast, shared by a whole church family. For most churches now it is a symbolic supper, a taking of a morsel of bread and a sip from a cup as a sign of our belonging to Christ's risen, redemptive body and of our unity with our Christian brothers and sisters everywhere; a healing, redemptive act of our whole body and soul which unites us more closely to Jesus Christ as the branch to the vine. But shouldn't every bite of food and every cup we drink through the day be considered as God's special gift to us, which is actually the gift of the energy of light through the fruits and meat of the earth? Isn't this food meant to bring us not only the life of the earth but the divine energy of God along with it?

Shouldn't all food we take also bind us more closely to our brothers and sisters who share this strength from God and help bring us to our nourishment as well as our brothers and sisters who are in desperate need of nourishment? Should it not awaken us and enliven us to their urgent need? Might there be healing of many of our eating and digestive problems if we thought of each bite of food as similar to that of Holy Communion in that God is offering us renewed life and love?

This does not mean we need to eat our meals with self-conscious solemnity. Anyone who has ever been to a Passover seder supper knows that there is warm laughter, joking, and fellowship along with the deep purposefulness. The Last Supper that Jesus shared with his disciples in the upper room *was* a Passover supper, and we can be sure that, even though he knew that it was the night before his death, there was good cheer and warmth and smiling closeness in that upper room. (Count how often Jesus uses the word *joy* as he talks to his disciples that night at supper in the Gospel of John.)

So we can eat our food, all our food, whether alone or

with others, with gratitude, joy, awe, expectancy, and expanding love for others because it is God who gives us life with every bite. With this in mind, we will begin to notice change in what we put into our bodies. Our bodies will joyously respond to this new approach to eating, and our nourishment will become a holy act. There will be holy and wholistic changes in our health.

Working

Oh send out thy light and thy truth; let them lead me.
—Psalm 43:3

We are to grow up in every way into him who is the head, into Christ, from whom the whole body, joined and knit together by every joint . . . , when each part is working properly, makes bodily growth and upbuilds itself in love.

—Ephesians 4:15-16

All forms of our working involve our bodies. Whether teaching, cleaning, writing, repairing, building, nursing, gardening, organizing, driving, counseling, or cooking, our bodies are at work. Within our work it is healthful to give a friendly, encouraging thought to the parts of the body especially involved, just the way we would encourage our child or a good friend.

For example, if your eyes are especially involved, every now and then mentally thank them, visualizing the river of renewing light flowing to them from deep within your body. Occasionally put your palms gently over your eyes for a few seconds and let them be refreshed by picturing green hills and valleys or letting each eye slowly breathe in and out.

If your hands, feet, or legs are heavily used, occasionally touch them (either with your hands or with your thoughts) with friendly gratitude and picture God's rivers of light flowing into them. In the midst of their work, if you are aware of fatigue and you cannot stop at that moment to rest, speak inwardly to them, thank them, encourage them, and express confidence in them. Someone recently told me of a woman lost in a wilderness area who was able to keep her exhausted, blistered feet moving only because she kept lovingly talking to them and praising them for each step.

If hard, complex thinking and communicating is required, try to take at least a few seconds ahead of time to relax and see your whole body and then the head area permeated with flowing light. Let the very brain cells be washed in God's river of light.

Be sensitive to signals of distress and discomfort from your body during work. These are probably telling you about emotional wounds and stress as well as physical. If possible, listen immediately and see if emotional healing or change in the work pattern is possible. If that is not possible at the moment, speak to the signal: "Yes, I hear you. I promise I'll get back to you as soon as possible." Be sure to keep that promise later and get in touch with the signal and its significance.

Recreation, Exercise, Sexual Activity, Sports, Celebration

Blessed are the people who know the festal shout, . . . who exult in thy name all the day. . . . For thou art the glory of their strength.
—Psalm 89:15-17

The Lord takes pleasure in his people. . . . Let the faithful exult in glory; let them sing for joy on their couches.
—Psalm 149:4-5

Daily Life in Prayer with Our Bodies

Let everything that breathes praise the Lord!
—Psalm 150:6

Yes, these are holy acts of prayer if our recreation, sexuality, and exercise are grateful, ecstatic manifestations of God's love for us, in us, and through us! While walking, running, stretching, dancing, swimming, or bicycling, remain in delighted, loving contact with your body, now released in full power. Be intentional and glad in these powers. Let your motions not be jerky or abrupt, but smooth, flowing, elastic. As you move, think of the joints as if they were made of flowing light, expanding, moving, stretching with fluidity. As you breathe deeply, think of each breath bringing new life to every organ and cell.

In the sexual activity of your loving, do not fear the torrent of feeling which is released, or, if aware of fear, ask for healing. Sexual activity is not merely a gift of God's love, but an actual participation in God's passionate love for all creation. What we feel is only a tiny spark to what God feels for us all. Trust your body to be your loving guide as you are released into the realm of sensory power. Within loving commitment, this is an act of healing, and an act of the highest holiness. Afterwards, as you thank God, also thank your body for channeling to you the gift of God's own delight.

Sleeping

In peace I will both lie down and sleep; for thou alone, O Lord, makest me dwell in safety.
—Psalm 4:8

For [God] gives to his beloved sleep.
—Psalm 127:2

125

As with sexual activity, lying down and releasing the consciousness into sleep is an act of trust towards our bodies, within the embrace of God. And the deeper our trust, the more fully God is able to give to us.

Before releasing ourselves to sleep, it is nurturing to stretch the body fully and gently to listen to the signals the body is giving to us now and through the day, and to think of ways by which we can more sensitively respond to these needs. Are our bodies reporting some inner hurt? Are our bodies telling us of some growing empowerment? Let them be touched by the healing of Christ. This can be part of every evening prayer, no matter how short. If we are anxious about those we love, we can commit them to the hands of Christ or visualize them surrounded by God's healing light.

If any bodily parts seem especially tired or strained in any way, touch them with love and let them breathe and drink of God's light flowing through them. Perhaps think of one of your organic systems and thank it for its work, asking God for its renewal.

Let your body lead you into sleep knowing that, though your surface consciousness is sleeping, your eyes closed, your blood pressure dropping, your sensory awareness dimmed, nevertheless, your body, the faithful companion, quietly works on, closely in touch with the enfolding life of God, restoring and sustaining your whole being. As Brother Lawrence said more than three hundred years ago in his little book, *The Practice of the Presence of God*: "Those who have the gale of the Holy Spirit go forward even in sleep."

If you cannot sleep, try not to be anxious or guilty. Trust your body to take what sleep it needs. It is not a time for vigorous, intense thinking, but a time for nurturing prayer of the profoundest quality. Let the light of God flow over and through you as suggested in earlier meditations. Let every bodily part breathe slowly and gently. Abandon your full weight trustfully to the bed, letting it hold you. Think of yourself as cradled in God's arms, as a father or mother holds a little relaxed child. Let each of your worries (even worry about worry) also be held in God's arms, resting on God's strength. Even if you do not sleep for hours, this resting trustfully upon God is giving you what sleep gives.

There is no better prayer for our sleepless times than the Sixty-third Psalm.

> My mouth praises thee with joyful lips,
> When I think of thee upon my bed,
>   and meditate on thee in the watches of the night;
> for thou hast been my help,
>   and in the shadow of thy wings I sing for joy.
> My soul clings to thee;
> thy right hand upholds me.
>
> —Psalm 63:5-8

Christ and Our Transformed Bodies

The memorial service for our ninety-one-year-old father was held several weeks after his death. As the family sat together after the service, the ashes of his cremated body were brought to the house. As we talked, I held the surprisingly heavy cardboard container, holding it close as we shared warm thoughts and memories of our father's life. None of us doubted that his gentle, generous spirit and his keenly probing mind still lived within God's love. But what about the precious body, the body through which he had smiled at us, hugged us, showed us his love in so many ways? Was this heavy cardboard container the last we would see of his body? Was this the last way we could ever touch or hold him bodily?

When we die, do we say goodbye forever to these friends, our bodies? What do the creeds mean when they speak of the resurrection of the body? Do they mean anything?

Some Christians believe that at the moment of death we will be given new heavenly bodies prepared for us in the next world. Others believe that on the last day these actual physical cells and organs which are laid in the grave will be raised and join our souls in heaven. Still others are sure that in our resurrected life we won't need any bodies at all, that we will forever be bodiless spirits living in incorporeal light.

I wonder if any of these interpretations are really very helpful to us. I find it hard to believe that every physical cell of mine (which will have long since separated and returned to earth and water) will be gathered together as a revived corpse. I find it equally a problem to think of stepping out of this body and then stepping into a new, strange one, rather like walking out of my house and walking into one I had never seen before. But neither do I believe that we will float around forever as formless vapor. Every one of the great religious faiths witness to a real body of light, a resurrected body. When writing to the church in Corinth, Paul speaks specifically and firmly of a spiritual *body* (1 Cor. 15). And certainly the risen Christ was no vapor!

What *is* a spiritual body? When I read and hear the accounts of persons who have had a near-death or an out-of-body experience (and remembering some experiences of that sort I had some years ago), I am impressed by the fact that one almost always feels definitely *embodied*. And the body in which one finds one's self feels real and natural, though far more free, swift, and strong. And though one has left a physical body lying on the bed, on the operating table, or in the wrecked car, the released body is one's *own*, not a new one handed over at the last minute by an angel! After going through the transition of death (and maybe in the very act of dying), I believe we will find we have not left our beloved bodies behind, but will instead find them with us still in a new, empowered way.

I have just finished talking on the telephone with a friend, a scientist, whose mother has just died. "How do you think of your mother?" I asked. "How do you visualize her?"

He answered, musingly, "I see her as a person of earth and water who has become a person of air and light. I think of her as still in her body, but that body is manifesting itself in another way, a way of swifter vibratory energy."

Our physical cells and molecules through which our bodies manifest themselves in this life will separate and return to earth or ash. *But this has always been true of our bodies, even while in this life!* We have already survived many physical deaths. Many times our cells have undergone change, and the old cells have died and been cast off. The physical body we have now is *not* the same as the physical body we had as embryos, babies, teenagers. But the changes happened so gradually that we hardly realize our physical bodies have died many times. But in spite of this, we know we have always been within the same body because the *real* body is the central, organizing energy within and permeating us through which we manifest ourselves in any dimension to which God calls us. And this particular, creative, central *act* which is our body is forever part of us and partner to us throughout life, manifesting its energy through our beating hearts, our brain waves, our orderly organic rhythms. As we move through death, this essential bodily energy never leaves us. And as we continue to grow in God's love, into more brightness, more joy, more responsiveness, we will still be partnered to our bodies, though their appearance and activity will be as different from what they are now as the oak tree differs from the acorn and the Olympic athlete differs from the embryo!

We will not experience any sense of fragmentation or separation between body and spirit then. We will experience a unity that is almost unimaginable to us now. The unity of God's light flashing and flowing without break from spirit to form and from form to spirit will have become the passionate oneness that was always God's will, God's longing for us.

But we need not wait for death to begin to experience the healing of this fragmentation which has been both our burden and our sadness. Resurrected life can begin now! Christianity is the daily and deepening love relationship with the living Jesus Christ through whom we experience most deeply the passion of God's healing love.

Any form of Christianity which is not incarnational, which does not celebrate "the Word made flesh," which tries to separate us from our own bodies, the bodies of our communities, the body of this earth is not the Christianity of our Lord Jesus Christ. In Christ the walls of hostility, the walls of division and fragmentation within us and among us are encountered, touched, healed. The Christ moves lovingly and with power through our closed doors and confronts our frightened selves, just as the risen Christ moved through the closed doors of the house where the disciples hid. And the loving hands were stretched out, showing the wounds that were not wasted or swallowed up in glory but that had become sources of redemptive love.

If we take those hands stretched out to us, our own wounds of body and spirit become to us no longer signs of hopeless pain but also sources of new-springing love! Then, abiding in Christ's risen body, we begin now to become a new creation, an empowered unity. As Agnes Sanford expresses it:

> He is now living, a Presence, a Personality, yet a Being so infinite in power that He can go through the doors of our bodies and enter into us and abide in us. . . .
> As we become more and more filled with His life, it

may come to us to change our prayer and to say, "Lord Jesus Christ, receive me into Thy own glorified Being that I may abide in Thee." Words are not great enough to describe that sense of walking about in a body of light that . . . is His light.[21]

Paul makes the same witness when he writes to the church in Corinth: "While we are still in this tent [our mortal body], we sigh with anxiety; not that we would be unclothed [leave our bodies], but that we would be further clothed, so that what is mortal may be swallowed up by life" (2 Cor. 5:4).

What a glorious way of expressing what we deeply long for, "that what is mortal may be swallowed up by life"! The point is that we need not wait for death to have our soma, our whole selves swallowed up by life. It can begin this day, in each eager, responding cell of our bodies, if we begin to let God's love shine through our eyes, touch through our hands, speak through our voices, and pray through our praying. For this is the meaning of resurrection.

> All things have become light, never again to set;
> And the setting has believed in the rising.
> This is the new creation.
> —St. Clement, third century

Appendix 1:
Guidelines for Entering
Depth Meditations
and Prayer

As we enter into depth visualizing prayer and meditation, we experience God's love in new and powerful ways. Also, we encounter our own deep selves in new and unexpected ways. The following guidelines are offered as suggestions so that depth prayer may be experienced in positive, creative ways, whether you are alone or in a group situation.

It is wise and helpful to begin the meditation by focusing on the loving nurture of God who surrounds and embraces you. You might begin with scripture reading, singing or listening to music, thinking about Jesus or looking at a picture of him. In this way, your meditation is put under the protection of God through Christ who longs for our deep healing.

Remind yourself that God understands your wounds, your hesitations, your fears, and does not demand instant complete trust and surrender. God is far more patient than we are and will not give up on you or leave you. Trust grows slowly. Take as much time as you need, and do not push yourself or allow anyone else to do so.

Remember that God honors your freedom. At any time during a meditation, feel free to change the imagery and the symbolism. Feel free to close off inwardly the voice of the leader and move into some other form of prayer or meditation.

Be willing to move as slowly as you please through any meditation. Stop at any point you wish and focus on that moment.

If you are aware of growing discomfort or anxiety or you are experiencing more pain with any meditation than you wish to feel, feel free to leave the meditation. You are not "letting God down." God is not a torturer. You can pray in some other way. If you feel guided to do so, you can return later.

Remember that the love of God can come to us in many different symbolic ways: a feeling of love and comfort; an inner picture of Jesus; a sense of light; the feeling of strength holding you; a warmth within or around your body; an inner, spoken word; a strong feeling of authentic guidance or moral decision. Be flexible, and let God come to you in the way that is right for *you*, whatever others may be experiencing.

If you don't feel any special sense of presence or any strong inner symbols, be assured that God is near you always. God's closeness to us and love for us does not depend on inner symbols or emotional or sensory awareness. Sometimes we need just to rest on the faith that God hears and is near. You are still healing and growing.

If you become aware of inner defenses, closed doors, walls, or blocks, do not try to break them down or tear them off. Never do inner violence to yourself in your spiritual growing or let anyone else do so to you. These inner defenses have kept us strong during the years of our vulnerable woundedness. Visualize the living Christ encountering your defenses with full transforming love. God understands that our walls and closed doors are really part of ourselves, part of our deep pain and fear, and God will heal them with tenderness.

If you are aware of inner self-condemnation, self-judgment, scorn, and contempt, know that this is not the voice of God, but rather the voice of your wounded self playing judge! Ask God to heal that part of you also.

You may find that you wish to weep quietly during the healing meditation. This is natural and a beautiful gift of self-release from God.

You may find that you wish to sleep briefly during the meditation. Do not assume (or let anyone else tell you) that this is an attempt to escape from God and the self-encounter because you sleep. It may be that God gently lays your surface consciousness to rest so that your deep self may be reached more deeply and tenderly.

If you feel restless and uncomfortable during depth meditation, it may be a signal that God calls you to prayer through bodily motion or walking.

Occasionally talk over your meditation experiences with a trusted group or a friend. Listen, and reflect on their responses. It is helpful and healthful to have persons with whom we share accountability during our spiritual growing.

Reflect on the "fruits of the Spirit" growing in your life. Over a period of time, do there seem to be any real changes resulting from your healing meditations? Is there more understanding and compassion for others? Is there more awareness of your own needs, limits, wounds, powers? Is there a sense of something moving and stretching within you? Are there any changes in your health, your relationships, your values and choices?

Let God call you *out* as well as *in*. We are continually growing, as we are with any vital relationship. Prayer methods that may have been releasing and helpful in the past may become prisons of your spirit if adhered to rigidly. Keep alert and attentive to inner guidance toward new forms of prayer and relating to God.

Appendix 2:
Guidelines for Leading
Depth Prayer for Others

The minister, lay leader, or group facilitator who leads others in depth healing prayer has a responsibility to be aware of the needs of group members at all times. It is a time of great openness, vulnerability, and self-encounter for the group members. The following suggestions are made in a spirit of respect for the dignity, uniqueness, and freedom of each person participating and for the sovereignty of God, who is the true leader of any prayer group.

Give some thought to the physical setting of the meditation. Is there a warm atmosphere? Are the chairs reasonably comfortable, or are there rugs and pillows for lying on the floor so that group members can relax their bodies? Is there a source of fresh air? Reasonable quiet? Is there a center of beauty or light on which people can focus if they wish, such as a lighted candle, a flower, or a picture?

Allow plenty of time for the bond of trust to grow between you and the group members and among the group members before you guide them into depth healing prayer. In an ongoing prayer group, you may wish to meet several times before you go into depth. In a workshop or retreat, allow for at least a couple of hours for the group to share thoughts and feelings with you and each other and to feel comfortable together before you move into depth meditation.

Spend some time at the beginning sharing thoughts and meditating on the love of God, perhaps using scripture readings and some hymn singing. It is important that group members feel that their depth meditation is under the guidance and protection of God's love. Discuss the alternative ways and symbols through which God's presence may be known.

Be sure that at all times you are using nonthreatening, nonjudgmental imagery.

Make it clear and explicit at the beginning of *each* meditation that members of the group are free at any time to leave the room if they wish, to change the imagery and symbolism for themselves, to withdraw quietly from the proposed meditation, to move into some other form of prayer, to go to sleep if they wish. Sleep is not necessarily an act of avoidance. It may be a God-given sleep so that deep parts of the self may be reached more compassionately.

Remind your group members that they are free to stop and focus for themselves at any point of the meditation. They do not have to "keep up" with the others or with your voice.

Reassure them that if they do not feel any special presence of God that God is still completely close to them. Reassure them that if they become aware of inner blocks or doors that seem closed, they need not do violence on themselves. God will gradually heal these walls and blocks.

Remind your group before a memory-healing meditation that if the memory is too painful at present to encounter, it is enough to ask the living Christ to walk into that memory of the past without forcing the group members to go there also.

Do not urge your group to surrender completely to God, to release everything, to make a leap of faith. Most people are still somewhat afraid of God, and most people have deep unfaced wounds. Trust grows slowly as healing gradually deepens. Assure your group members that small amounts of faith and trust are enough to begin with and that God understands and has compassion.

Move through your meditation very slowly. Allow times of silence between each group of suggested imagery.

At the close of a meditation, give some suggested "grounding" images. Suggest that the group members become aware of the room in which they sit and the loving presence of others around them before they open their eyes. Allow a few moments of silence, perhaps with stretching and gentle face massage before talking together.

Suggest some time for group sharing and reflection. Encourage the members to discuss their experiences if they wish, especially any discomfort they may have felt.

Never *require* members to share their thoughts and experiences. Some may wish to reflect in silence. Help them to feel perfectly comfortable about keeping silence if they prefer.

If anyone seems to feel wistful or left out because he or she did not have the same kinds of experiences the others did, reassure everyone that each person's experience is unique, that God encounters us all in different ways, and that it is the *fruits* of the meditation that count more than the symbolic experiences within meditation.

Listen carefully to all group reactions about the imagery used, the timing, and the length of the meditation. You are all sharing this together as an experience of healing and growth.

Be sure that you, the leader, also have a chance to experience the meditations as a group member occasionally, with someone else taking the role of leader.

Notes

1. *Meditations with Julian of Norwich*, versions by Brendan Doyle (Santa Fe, NM: Bear & Company, 1983), pp. 29, 95, 93.

2. Madeleine L'Engle, *A Winter's Love* (New York: Balantine Books, 1984), pp. 152-53.

3. Elizabeth Noble, *Childbirth with Insight* (Boston: Houghton Mifflin Company, 1983), pp. 8-9.

4. Ron DelBene with Herb Montgomery, *Breath of Life* (Minneapolis: Winston Press, 1981), pp. 15-16.

5. Julian of Norwich, pp. 123, 82, 85.

6. Susan Griffin, *Pornography and Silence* (New York: Harper & Row, Publishers, 1981; New York: Harper & Row, Colophon Books, 1982), pp. 86-87.

7. Gilbert K. Chesterton, *Orthodoxy* (New York: John Lane Company, 1909), pp. 180-81.

8. *Meditations with Mechtild of Magdeburg*, versions by Sue Woodruff (Santa Fe, NM: Bear & Company, 1982), p. 89.

9. dia r. thompson, "Anger," in Susan E. Browne et al., eds., *With the Power of Each Breath* (Pittsburg: Cleis Press, 1985), pp. 79-81.

10. Deborah Abbott, "This Body I Love," in Browne, et al., pp. 246-47.

11. Bernie S. Siegel, *Love, Medicine, & Miracles* (New York: Harper & Row, Publishers, 1986), pp. 120-123.

12. Norman Cousins, *The Healing Heart* (New York: W. W. Norton & Company, 1983; New York: Avon Books, 1984), pp. 188-90.

13. Leslie Weatherhead, *Psychology, Religion and Healing* (Nashville: Abingdon Press, 1952), pp. 237-38.

14. Henri J. M. Nouwen, *The Wounded Healer* (Garden City, NJ: Doubleday and Company, 1972; Garden City, NJ: Image Books, 1979), p. 94.

15. Elizabeth Goudge, *The Joy of the Snow* (New York: Coward, McCann & Geoghegan, 1974), p. 222.

16. *Meditations with Hildegard of Bingen*, versions by Gabriele Uhlein (Santa Fe, NM: Bear & Company, 1983), pp. 77, 78.

17. Hildegard of Bingen, pp. 91, 107.

18. Agnes Sanford, *Creation Waits* (Plainfield, NJ: Logos International, 1978), p. 7.

19. Matthew Fox, *Original Blessing* (Santa Fe, NM: Bear & Company, 1983), pp. 37-38.

20. Pierre Teilhard de Chardin, *Hymn of the Universe* (New York: Harper & Row, Publishers, 1965), pp. 63-65.

21. Agnes Sanford, *Behold Your God* (Saint Paul, MN: Macalester Park Publishing Company, 1958), p. 125.

Suggested Readings

Creative Living and Praying

Browne, Susan E., et al., eds., *With the Power of Each Breath: A Disabled Woman's Anthology*. Pittsburgh: Cleis Press, 1985.

Campbell, Peter A. and McMahon, Edwin M. *Bio-Spirituality: Focusing As a Way to Grow*. Chicago: Loyola University Press, 1985.

DelBene, Ron and Montgomery, Herb. *Breath of Life: Discovering Your Breath Prayer*. Minneapolis: Winston Press, 1981.

———. *Hunger of the Heart*. Minneapolis: Winston Press, 1983.

DeMello, Anthony. *Sadhana: A Way to God, Christian Exercise in Eastern Form*. St. Louis: Institute of Jesuit Sources, 1978.

Doyle, Brendan, ed. *Meditations with Julian of Norwich*. Santa Fe, NM: Bear and Company, 1983.

Grassi, Joseph A. *Changing the World Within: The Dynamics of Personal and Spiritual Growth*. Mahwah, NJ: Paulist Press, 1986.

Kelsey, Morton T. *The Other Side of Silence: A Guide to Christian Meditation*. Mahwah, NJ: Paulist Press, 1976.

Savary, Louis M. and Berne, Patricia H. *Prayerways: For Those Who Feel Discouraged or Distraught, Frightened or Frustrated, Angry or Anxious, Powerless or Purposeless, Over-Extended or Under-Appreciated, Burned Out or Just Plain Worn Out*. New York: Harper and Row, Publishers, 1984.

Stahl, Carolyn. *Opening to God: Guided Imagery Meditation on Scripture*. Nashville: The Upper Room, 1977.

Whitehead, James D. and Whitehead, Evelyn E. *Seasons of Strength: New Visions of Adult Christian Maturing.* New York: Doubleday and Co., Inc., 1984.

Healing: General

Cousins, Norman. *The Healing Heart: Antidotes to Panic and Helplessness.* New York: W. W. Norton and Co., 1983.

Kelsey, Morton T. *Healing and Christianity.* New York: Harper and Row, Publishers, 1976.

Linn, Dennis and Matthew, and Fabricant, Sheila. *Praying with One Another for Healing.* Mahwah, NJ: Paulist Press, 1984.

Locke, Steven and Colligan, Douglas. *The Healer Within: The New Medicine of Mind and Body.* New York: E. P. Dutton, 1986.

Sanford, John A. *Healing and Wholeness.* Mahwah, NJ: Paulist Press, 1977.

Siegel, Bernard S. *Love, Medicine and Miracles.* New York: Harper and Row, Publishers, 1986.

Wagner, James K. *Blessed to Be a Blessing,* Nashville: The Upper Room, 1980.

Inner Healing

Kelsey, Morton T. *Christo-Psychology.* New York: Crossroad Publishing Co., 1982.

Linn, Dennis and Matthew, and Fabricant, Sheila. *Prayer Course for Healing Life's Hurts.* Mahwah, NJ: Paulist Press, 1983.

Manning, Brennan. *Stranger to Self-Hatred.* Denville, NJ: Dimension Books, 1982.

Miller, William A. *Make Friends with Your Shadow: How to Accept and Use Positively the Negative Side of Your Personality.* Minneapolis: Augsburg Publishing House, 1981.

Wuellner, Flora S. *Prayer, Stress, and Our Inner Wounds.* Nashville: The Upper Room, 1985.

Spirituality and Sexuality

Donnelly, Dorothy H. *Radical Love: Toward a Sexual Spirituality.* Minneapolis: Winston Press, 1984.

Kelsey, Morton T. and Kelsey, Barbara. *Sacrament of Sexuality*. Warwick, NJ: Amity House, Inc., 1986.

Nelson, James B. *Embodiment: An Approach to Sexuality and Christian Theology*. Minneapolis: Augsburg Publishing House, 1979.

Tyrrell, Thomas J. *Urgent Longings: Reflections on the Experience of Infatuation, Human Intimacy, and Contemplative Love*. Natick, MA: Affirmation Books, 1980.

Approaches to Stress Management

Benson, Herbert and Klipper, Miriam Z. *The Relaxation Response*. New York: Avon Books, 1976.

Benson, Herbert and Proctor, William. *Beyond the Relaxation Response*. New York: Berkley Publishing Group, 1985.

Mason, L. John. *Guide to Stress Reduction*, revised edition. Berkeley, CA: Celestial Arts Publishing Co., 1986.

Rassieur, Charles L. *Stress Management for Ministers*. Philadelphia: Westminster Press, 1982.

Prayer and Our Earth

Fox, Matthew. *Original Blessing*. Santa Fe, NM: Bear and Company, 1983.

Sanford, Agnes. *The Creation Waits*. Los Angeles: Bridge Publications, Inc., 1977.

Teilhard de Chardin, Pierre. *Hymn of the Universe*. New York: Harper and Row, Publishers, 1969.

Uhlein, Gabriele, ed., *Meditations with Hildegard of Bingen*. Santa Fe, NM: Bear and Company, 1982.

About the Author

Flora Slosson Wuellner is an adjunct member of the faculty at Pacific School of Religion in Berkeley, California. She is an ordained minister in the United Church of Christ and has served churches in Chicago, Idaho, and Wyoming.

Ms. Wuellner has been a leader of retreats and conferences for almost twenty years. She is the author of several books, her most recent being *Prayer, Stress, and Our Inner Wounds*.